Bargepoles an

A new life aboard a narrow boat

Prologue (Linda's writings in Italics)

It was a lovely Christmas evening...music playing in the Frenchgate centre Doncaster, crowds milling around happily, shop assistants were dressed as elves while we debated on a present for his mother – that was when the mobile phone call came.....'Oh Mrs Clover, I'm so glad I've got you....Bodhran's on fire....it's serious'. As we waited outside the railway station for Sarah the marina manager to collect us I felt sick and thought back to our monumental decision, some months earlier to sell up everything and move to a life living on a narrow boat. In fact you need to go back even further – to a river boat called 'Sea Spray' or a hired narrow boat called 'Devon' but if you ask us where it all started, how the seeds were sown, why our thoughts turned from idle daydreams into compulsive urges you would get different answers from us both. When we ask each other, it is now obvious that in hindsight if our reasons for doing what we did had sprung up in the same way....then maybe, just maybe, we would never have done it at all. This explains to me why we did do it. Why we each made up our own minds that we wanted to do it - and why we did it. We both wanted to.

The Summer of 2012. The Opening of the Lock Gates.

"You must come down to Tewksbury and see what Annette and I have just bought"

It was David, one of Linda's two brothers and Annette his wife, both given to acts of supreme spontaneous madness but with hearts of gold.

"We have been out with friends of ours and they have one so we thought, let's buy one too...and buy it right now before we have the time to change our minds"

The following weekend Linda and I left our little white cottage in Camblesforth North Yorkshire for the three hour plus trip to Tewkesbury and the river Avon, barely believing what our hosts to-be had told us on the phone earlier that week.

We drove to their house in Cheltenham and then they took us to a small marina just outside Tewkesbury...it was a beautiful calm and sunny day.

And there she was....in all her glory...sitting beneath her bright blue awning with the sun on her fibreglass roof and the undulating waters of the Avon lapping gently at her bows...the 23ft river cruiser Sea Spray...one look at her sleek lines and the seeds were sown.

Sea Spray.

Laden with bags full of chicken, bread, ham, crackers, cheese, ale and wine we awaited with baited breath as the skipper carefully dismantled the awning, wound in the stern ropes and unlocked the cabin doors, the atmosphere was electric.

"Have you guys been out in her yet?" My question had the effect of catching two sets of rabbit eyes in a cars headlight.

"A couple of times" came back the skipper's response, "but don't worry we are getting the stern rail fixed on the insurance, the damage done to the bow was minimal and I'm sure I've got the hang of steering her now" David had his back to me and was kneeling down busy lifting the cratch plate exposing the single onboard. "Right that should do it" he said standing up and wiping his hands on his jeans... he almost sounded as if he knew what he had done.

The cratch plate back in its place we were welcomed aboard the vessel onto the slatted stern and then heads bowed into the relative coolness and shadow of the tiny galley. The gentle swaying and buffeting of the ropes tied on the mooring poles gave the impression that the 'Sea Spray' herself was anxious to be unfettered from the bounds of terra firma and let loose to roam with gay abandon the mighty Avon. With the 'girls' in the small kitchen unpacking the requisites for a picnic by the river upstream, David started Sea Sprays engine and in a haze of blue diesel smoke we made our way on a gentle bow wave into midstream and towards the very first lock of so many that Linda and I were destined to encounter.

I for one was immediately smitten, with the thrum of the boats tiny prop churning the waters below my feet and the gentle but somehow powerful forward motion of the tiny vessel fighting her way against the current, a feeling of utter freedom filled my senses. I breathed deeply the cold earthy smells, and marvelled at the scenes of nature at its most beautiful unfolding before me. Captivated by the sights you can only see of a river when you are on it, in it, each meandering bend offering up something new to take in, to devour. The contrasts between the black grey reflection of drifting clouds on the water's surface and then the blinding gold of the sun when it stabs a way through forcing a hand to your forehead to shield your eyes. On either side of Sea Sprays hull the banks glided leisurely by revealing the secret holes of voles buried deep within them, sunken tree trunks green with age and dense foliage, home to kingfishers, shelters for ducks and shadows for the huge fish idling in the deep waters below them.

"Take the wheel First Mate and I'll go below decks and get us a couple of beers" It was hard to know what sounded better to my ears on that glorious day, the skipper calling me 'First Mate', 'take the wheel' or 'I'll get us couple of beers'....but it was certainly a closely run thing. David disappeared into the small living area of the boat and left me on the decks cushioned seat completely in charge, the crew's very lives depended on my extremely limited seamanship and dubious skills at navigation....when you can reach heady speeds of up to 8 knots you should take nothing for granted...

I stood alone on the foredeck, one hand on the boats gear lever the other on the boats wheel, I could hear the muffled conversations below deck but that is all they were - 'muffled conversations' I had no time for such trivialities, another boat was fast approaching and its skipper waving to me from its wheelhouse obviously completely oblivious to the fact the boat *he* was approaching had a complete novice at its controls. We were soon to be alongside each other...was I on the right side of him? Did I have to sound my horn? If I steered too close would the bow waves smash into each other's keels and tip us over into the freezing waters? Or worst still would David spill my beer on his way up from the lower deck? I held myself in check as we drew alongside; gripping Sea Sprays wheel in both hands whilst the other boats 2 inch high wake battered our hull.

And then all of a sudden we were once again in calm waters, like ships that pass in the night, the waves had abated, the boat settled to her chug, chugging and a figure with an arm outstretched holding a glass of beer appeared from the shadows of the cabin... "Soon be at the first lock Kim" it said "Do you want me to take over?"....My response was as nonchalant as I could make it.... "Can do David, can do"

Minutes later it appeared through the warm hazy mist, less than 100 meters ahead, completely traversing the canal and totally blocking our path. A huge wall of what looked like mud covered vertical railway sleepers held together by massive rusting hinges, fountains of water seeped through jagged cracks in its contoured surfaces like the tears of a giant with his eyes tightly closed. So high above Sea Sprays bow that I had to crane my neck up to see heavily glossed black and white wooden balance beams spread themselves above the waters to reach each side of the canals concrete banks, a bastion of defiance against those who would attempt to move them, as very soon we would be.

The chug chugging of Sea Sprays engine slowed to an unnerving idling and in an eerie pregnant silence our skipper David steered us gently into the port bank and the concrete jetty topped with black painted bollards...at the bow Annette was up and ready with the stern ropes and with a well practiced skip she was on terra firma and bending over tying us up. Here we would draw breath and gather our nerve for soon unless another boat joined us we would enter the abyss completely alone. Just a few feet ahead and towering above us the monstrous lock gates were looking down with undisguised mocking its toothless mouth wide open ready and eager to swallow us whole..... *"You are before me now...there is no turning back"*.....and we were, and there wasn't.

 So there we sat looking aft for what seemed an age...no sign of another vessel, "Always good to go through the lock with another boat if you can" David's forlorn but hopeful voice bounced off the water's surface and echoed back at us from somewhere deep in the locks bowels....And then... "Well we can't stay here all day Annette, (yes we can, I distinctly remember thinking) untie us please darling and we'll go it alone". As he spoke I felt the slight tip of the boat as Annette alighted followed by the familiar chug chug as Sea Sprays engine spluttered into life, Annette gave a little outward shove to the boats bow and all at once we were heading out into midstream towards the gapping mouth of the vast concrete and wooden, all encompassing, water spitting beast...and certain death as far as I was concerned.

As we slowly approached the rapidly narrowing entrance the surrounding walls of grey concrete grew high above our heads and closer to our gunnels, Sea Spray appeared to shrink before our very eyes. Gradually the sun disappeared and the resulting shadows threw a cold gloomy veil around us. Silhouetted against what was left of the light I could just make out the form of Annette as she made her way up and forward along the tow path towards the lock and then she too disappeared from sight. The sounds from the boats engine seemed to grow in intensity as it bounced off the open gates and then we had passed them and were into the locks deep foreboding interior, a female voice came from somewhere above me and David was standing on the bow throwing up a rope for Annette to catch and tie up. We were now in it, we were at a standstill, we had entered the tail gates of our first lock and before us the mouth of the head gates were closed (although leaking heavily in places) against a weight of water impossible to imagine and best not to think about. I actually began to feel a bit calmer until Annette's voice rang out again shattering what little comfort I'd allowed myself "Don't forget to stay well away from the cill David, we don't want the boat upending and sinking when I'm ready to open the paddles"

After a short while and accompanied by female grunts, one side of the tail gates began to move, its 'door' slowly making its way through the deep and littered water to the centre of the canal, out of sight from us somewhere above our heads Annette was making her way to the other side of the lock and the other 'door' ….soon we would be totally closed in the locks chamber…Sea Spray and her motley crew, twelve feet below the canals natural surface and at the mercy of a zillion tons of water already trying to force its way through a badly leaking gate, spraying us completely with fine jets of cold and angry water.

The deed was done, the only sounds that of water splashing (it appeared to coming from everywhere) and the gentle idling of the boats engine amplified by the walls of algae and slime covered walls now entombing us. I looked up to see Annette peering down at us from a great height not quite sure if the flushed look and wide smile on her face was due to all her recent exertions or the fact that she was happy up there safely on terra firma and had us all at her mercy down here inches from a watery grave …..(*Get out off that one without my help if you can*)….and then her voice floated down but with far too much undisguised glee for my liking…

"I'm going to open the head gate paddles now guys…. hang on"… Did she mean 'hang on in a *time sense*, or hang on in a '*you need to hang on to something solid because you are all going to be tossed about like leaves in a whirlpool sense?* At the time I really was not sure.

And then all of a sudden the waters below us grew white with turbulence and the small jets from the gates above turned to raging torrents, Annette had opened the paddles. "This is where we have to make sure we keep off the cills" David's excited yell came to us over the thunderous sound of rushing waters and I was not fully convinced that it came from a sane man. As the Sea Spray was buffeted from side to side and her entire structure pushed up from below as if by the giant hand of Neptune himself we were slowly ascending on a current of whirling eddies and bubbling foam. I could now see why our senior crew members had insisted on us wearing life jackets...the seemingly innocuous took on a whole new look and falling into an operating lock would not be a good idea. We were gradually going up and the suns probing fingers had begun chasing away the shadows and warming our cold and damp faces. As the sounds and violent movements subsided we finally found ourselves within 'stepping off' distance to the locks concrete surface and Annette standing on it rope in hand. "Give me a hand with opening the tail gates and we'll go through and moor up at the nearest pub" I was off the boat and standing next to her before the echo of her voice had had a chance to die down..

Our first lock of many successfully negotiated!

A Brief History of the Canals

As early as AD.50 the Romans built the Fossdyke from Lincoln to the river Trent for drainage and navigation, they were also responsible for the Caer Dyke. In 1566 the Exeter Canal was completed, a notable waterway which bypassed a part of a river making navigation easier. This had the first 'pound 'locks in Britain equipped with lifting vertical gates. The 'mitre' gate which had V shaped gates held together by the water pressure was introduced in this country on the River Lee at Waltham Abbey. Some other early British canals are an improved section of the River Welland in Lincolnshire built in1670 and the Stroudwater Navigation in Gloucester built 1775-1779 and the Sankey canal in Lancashire opened in stages 1757-1773.

The great age of Canal building started with the construction of the Bridgewater Canal, being the initiative of the 3rd Duke of Bridgewater it was nowhere near the town of Bridgwater itself but in Worsley, North West Manchester. Completed in 1776 it was the catalyst of half a century of canal building.

Next there followed a so called 'Grand Cross' of canals which linked four great river basins in Britain, the Severn, the Mersey, the Humber and the Thames. There were two concentrated periods of canal building from 1759 to the early 1770's and from 1789 almost to the end of the eighteenth century. Although most of our canals are now safe from closure, few are used for transporting goods.

The Aire and Caulder Canal.

We were now cruising at a steady 4 knots, taking in the ever changing scenery as the Sea Spray carried us along at her own leisurely pace...(nobody on the river is or should be in any hurry to go anywhere)...we meandered between the banks, one minute thick with impenetrable foliage, the next open and expansive. You find a different world when travelling by boat - on the land the cows in the fields ignore you, too busy chewing the cud, the sheep stand with heads down oblivious to all but the lush grass at their hooves, in the far distance a lonely man sits upon a lonely tractor ploughing a lonely furrow to match the hundred or so he has already ploughed, the scattered buildings stand like the trees and bushes surrounding them, quiet, still and utterly blind to the world...on the water swans fearlessly approach hoping for the morsels that they know will be thrown for them, ducks laugh a quack quack as they paddle away, little orange legs a blur below the water's surface, herons with their bent necks and clumsy wings flapping in silhouette against a cloudless sky…and if you are lucky, really lucky you may catch the glossy blue and red darting figure of the majestic kingfisher flashing through the air and diving skilfully into the depths for its next meal barely leaving a ripple.

And the pub is just around the next bend….could it get any better?

The imposing 'Barge Inn' was situated a short distant back from the canals edge beyond an area of lush lawn dotted with wooden benches under gaily coloured parasols. In the lawns centre a lone flag depicting an old sailing ship fluttered high in the light breeze. There was only one vessel tied up at the landing stage affording David enough room to moor up at its aft (I was already talking *nautical* by this time). The Sea Spray's engine was killed and under David's skilled manipulations we gently drifted towards our temporary moorings. Annette charged me with the bow rope and when near enough I stepped onto terra firma (it is bad etiquette to have to jump from a boat) and made my way to the nearest mooring bollard where after a fashion I tied us up. The crew were ready to imbibe a tot of rum (wine or ale more likely) and we made our way to the Inn post haste.

A warm welcome greeted us from a man with a huge beard, a huge sweater and an even huger stomach standing behind a bar bedecked with lobster pots, brass bells and anchors.

The scene was set for the end of a wonderful day, one which has etched itself deeply in my memory, adding the seeds of thought that were in time to grow and blossom.

Types of Boat

Traditional Narrow boat.

Suitable for most narrow and broad canals and rivers. Up to 21.3m (70 feet) long (maximum length for most canals)

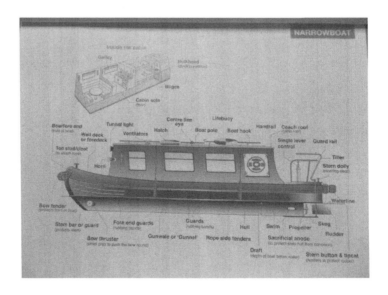

Canal Narrow boat- Semi Traditional or Cruiser Stern.

Usually have a larger rear deck, ideal for the family. Both types have steel hulls and are suitable for use on narrow canals.

Broad Beam and Dutch Barges.

Large craft, comfortable as a live-aboard vessel often used in mainland Europe.

Blacking the hull.

To protect the bottom section of the boat under water and just above the water line it is necessary to 'black it' periodically. This protects the hull from rust, pitting, and rubbing i.e. through locks, other boats, banks, etc. and will obviously extend its life. To do this the vessel needs to be taken out of the water and there are three ways to accomplish this.

1. Dry Dock – the boat is floated into a chamber and the water removed.
2. Craning – a crane is used to lift it from the water.
3. Slipway Trailer – a tractor and trailer haul the boat up onto a slipway and out.

The third option being the most popular due to costs.

There are generally 2 types of blacking 'paints' available – Bituminous or Epoxy. Of the two Bituminous is the cheaper with a requirement to repaint every 2-3 years…Epoxy paint is dearer with a longer 'life' of up to 6 years. It is important to remember that if the hull has previously been treated with bituminous paint this will have to be stripped down to the bare metal (shot blasting) if Epoxy paint is preferred which of course could be an expensive procedure.

Monday 15th April 2013.

What a day!!…we got to Sowerby Bridge around 12.30, drove down a very cobbled street and parked. The lady at Shire Cruisers told us to have lunch and get back around 13.45. We went to lovely pub, had a tuna melt and I got the chance to fuss a wonderful pair of great Danes. We got back to the boat and unpacked. The Devon is a lovely vessel – very small 25 ft long and compact but ideal for us just starting out for our first venture on a boat. I must admit I was very nervous about learning and using the locks!! We had a nice young lad, who took us through the boat showing us how to set up the table and the bed; he also took us through Health and Safety. What neither of us realised is that although they take you through the first three locks, they do not stay on board with you. We were nervous but soon mastered the art of steering. Prior to starting we had had an introductory talk with the wife of the couple who own Shire boats where routes were discussed and explained. We had also met a couple who were taking out another narrow boat, The Oxford. About fifteen minutes after leaving Sowerby Bridge, The Oxford caught up with us. They seemed to be going much faster; they kept slowing down to let us get ahead but always seemed to be at our stern. We got to the first locks where three men from Shire Boats were waiting for us to take both us and The Oxford through the locks. Kim steered us in – with instruction called out by one of the men – for the first lock. I stayed on the boat whilst he operated the lock. Everything went well and I was told to turn to starboard out of the gates and moor up before the second lock. It was a very windy day and as I began to turn – assisted by another man from Shire Boats who apparently was learning the 'job' – the wind 'took the boat, turned me completely round and I rammed the bank, head on! He jumped off and pulled us into the bank, but for a while I was really panicking! After that I decided it would be sensible for both of us to learn how to operate a lock, nothing at all to do with not wanting to repeat steering the boat through a lock again!! I found out I actually enjoyed doing the locks. We were shown different types of lock with the third being a key operated guillotine lock, then finally we were on our own! We moored up and The Oxford passed us, we didn't want them shadowing us and it seemed, judging by the size of their bow wave, they wanted to go faster. We got to our first lock alone, I took my ratchet key and got to work – I managed it perfectly. Shire boats man had been pleased that I had understood the logic of a lock and I operated the two locks easily. I was rather proud and enormously relieved!

We set off again and headed into Elland, it was quite strange, an industrial area but with a lot of warehouses boarded-up. There were broken windows, graffiti, floating debris and rubbish shadowing the towpath. It felt quite threatening and we got to the third lock with the light fading, worried that we weren't going to find anywhere suitable to moor up and aware we couldn't navigate in the dark. We finally moored up in front of the lock during which Kim completely lost it. I think it was a mixture of going too fast and unable to straightaway correct the way we were going. Anyway, we eventually righted ourselves and decided to tie up just ahead in front of The Oxford who had arrived there ahead of us. Kim moved us into the last space and they helped us tie up.

Exhausted, aching and weary I attempted to wash in the minute bathroom banging my elbows on all four walls in the process, following which armed with torches – as

recommended by Kim for the return journey – we made
our way along the tow path to the nearest pub!

Later back aboard Devon I had a lovely ten minutes
outside leaning against the taff rail, sipping wine and
looking out at the dark, the shadows and listening to the
sounds of the night. Kim meanwhile was sorting out
inside the boat, putting up the table and readying the
cabin for our first evening in. One thing to add is –
operating a lock whilst satisfactory in a weird way, is
very, very physical. Anyone who thinks it is a nice relaxed
time has not operated a lock before!!!!!

It was difficult to look forward to initially, not really a
holiday more a 'driving test' - now sitting in Devon, Plebs
on T.V. and a red wine in front of me, I thought I had
passed the test and the boat had become a friend not a
hurdle. I was very tired but a nice tired and I was looking

forward to the days/nights ahead – it was now time to batten down the hatches me hearties and lay our heads on our berths!

P.S. We had both had our panic attacks navigating Devon and we would undoubtedly have more but for now......we were on our own.

It was a strange night mixed with vivid dreams, the sound of rain hitting the boat and the thud as the boat hit the towpath! After lying awake listening for what seemed an age, I drifted off to sleep to be awoken by a crash as the The Oxford hit us as they attempted to leave. I washed and dressed using our tiny sink again and was ready before they had manage to leave, with Kim commenting " I thought they were going to take us with them!" We had a cup of tea outside enjoying the freshness of the early morning then I tidied the cabin while Kim completed his checks ready for the day ahead. By the

time we approached the lock The Oxford was nowhere to be seen. We negotiated the next two locks and I was secretly pleased with the way I managed them – I never thought I would and it is a massive relief mixed with a tinge of pride that I can. After the two locks we navigated a section of canal through a forest, it was so beautiful with the sun filtering through the trees that we moored up for and tea and bacon sandwiches. After a lovely interlude sitting outside in the sun listening to the birds and various animals rustling about in the trees we set off for the three locks before Brighouse. We negotiated the locks, the second was so difficult to move Kim had to leave the deck and help get things started, we had decided after looking at turning places on the map to 'turn' in the Brighouse basin and head back slowly. We approached the third lock and I set off noticing a new boat coming up astern. This lock was even worse than the second and I struggled to get any movement at all, a particularly hard shove giving me a pinging feeling in my chest. Hearing shouts I glanced behind me and decided I was probably hallucinating and had created a vision of a boat populated by several large brawny men. As the vessel came to a stop four or five men had emerged and with comments of 'just you leave it to us love' took over and the rest of the lock was easy. It culminated with the necessity of me crossing their boat – The Duke of York Community Initiative made up of a rugby club giving under privileged children a narrow boat ride on the canal - it couldn't have been better timing for me. We set off and entered Brighouse tailed by them and thought we would moor up just before the basin. The wind had been increasing in strength all morning and before we could tie up it caught us and using the boat as a sail sent us head on to the bank. After help from a basin 'official' and some other narrow boat owners we finally tied up when we were then rammed by The Duke of York, also caught out by the wind.

We were excited to have reached our first destination and were full of plans for shopping, finding a pub....we don't usually do it in that order...and enjoying life 'aboard' when we met our neighbours, an elderly couple moored behind us. Like the 'oracle' of 'doom and gloom' they regaled us with happy stories of kids cutting mooring ropes, running on the roofs of boats and generally attacking any innocent boats moored there. The Oxford was already there on the other side of us and he did finally end by saying that with two of us we needn't worry. We had been told by the official who had helped us tie up that it would be unwise to move tonight

*as gale force winds were expected. After a discussion
with The Oxford of how to reach the water standby
around the corner we headed to Tesco's for toilets, coffee
and provisions. We came back to Devon, dumped the
shopping and headed to the nearby pub The Barge,
deciding, with the high winds now blowing the water into
sizable waves not to stop long there but to head back for
Cornish pasties and an early night, during which the
water and the wind pushed at the boat and I began to
feel pain as I breathed just around the site of the
'pinging' in my ribs earlier.*

I completed my daily checks on Devon re; oil, grease, weed box, prop and now felt almost relaxed. I worked out the central heating system aboard and started the engine to recharge the boats batteries, feeling like a boats skipper for the first time in my life – all I had to do now was to convince my motley crew, namely Linda.

We woke in the morning to continuing strong winds and decided we were right not to go any further but to head back to Sowerby. I was determinedly ignoring the pain in my ribs which was now making any movement agonising and saying to myself 'this isn't happening'. Kim wanted to reach the water standby and fill up before leaving. This was situated around a ninety degree corner about one hundred metres ahead of us. I slipped the ropes off the mooring pins and Kim started to steer her out again, the wind caught Devon completing a full circle and sending us further and further out into the basin. We were now in 'full panic mode' with our neighbours plus other officials shouting instructions across the choppy waters. Kim turned to me and shouted "she's not doing anything! I am steering but nothing is happening!!!" Suddenly, after spinning another full circle she began to come to life again. We headed for the bank, threw ropes to the spectators, realising that the businesses and apartment windows were full of people watching the show. We sat and I waited for the panic to subside, for my breath to come back and for the pain to ease a little when Kim quietly confided "No wonder she wouldn't steer – I'd forgotten to put her in gear!!".... (Old boating saying...No gear, No steer)...I just looked at him open mouthed. Despite my pleas and protestations that I wouldn't drink any water Kim was determined not to be defeated and to make it to the standby. With my heart in my mouth I slipped the ropes again and we set off completing a perfect manoeuvre (this time in gear) filled up with water, turned a perfect circle (this time intentionally) and headed back.

A Typical Narrow Boat Basin.

I finally had to admit to Kim the pain I was in and he helped me with the three locks before we decided to have an early stop in the middle of the forest we had loved yesterday morning. We also hoped I had strained a muscle and a rest would do it good.

Once we stopped I found alcohol and pain killers worked quite well, although my comment about not needing the water was ignored. I had a lazy afternoon sitting in the bow of the boat looking at the trees and sipping wine while Kim went for a walk up the towpath and found a pub. It was beautiful in the forest, full of birdsong and completely shut off from civilisation, but at night it was absolutely pitch dark. As we settled for the night I was worried about the pain I was in and was finding it hard to sleep when the storm that had been threatening hit us. Kim slept through the whole thing but I was convinced we would slip our moorings and end up sailing down the canal hit the bridge we could see in the distance and sink. The only way I knew we hadn't was that we repeatedly thudded against the bank! Kim's mooring pins and knots held us securely all night. In the morning I had to admit that I could not move, the pain was radiating across my chest and into my arms making moving and breathing agony. I very tearfully called Shire Boats and they were wonderful, driving someone down to us, finding us along the tow path and escorting us back to Sowerby Bridge. I sat in the cabin feeling a failure but in such pain I didn't care. Kim and the man from Shire Boats took us back through the locks to their moorings. I sat in the van whilst Kim emptied the boat and we set off for The Calderdale Royal Hospital where after doctors, nurses and x rays it was decided I had managed to crack three ribs. This ended our first trip – and somehow I still fell in love with narrow boating but it was a proper love, not a sunny afternoon holiday type love but an everyday problems, in sickness and in health and bad weather type love and I was determined to repeat the experience.

A Normal Life?

Arriving back home it took a while for my ribs to heal and despite my initial euphoria my confidence in our 'brave new life' had taken a beating and doubts began to creep in. As ever everyday life left me little time to realise that the psychological damage would remain for far longer than the physical unless properly dealt with. We avoided the subject for a while until another visit to my brothers in Cheltenham and another day out on Sea Spray brought everything to the fore again. It was a lovely day, bright, calm and sunny, meandering down the river, stopping for a coffee here, shopping down some quaint alleys there, a picnic and a drink at a club on the river's edge to finish the day that brought the dream alive again. It reminded me of the peace and tranquillity, the sheer pleasure to be found in a life afloat. It did not always mean pain, gale force winds, imminent sinking and - when you got carried away – death by drowning.

This was September time and for a few months now I had secretly been logging on to the narrow boat websites and viewing the boats for sale, poring over the descriptions and photos of interiors trying to fit us into each one and each time thoroughly convincing myself it was a perfect fit. Finally, after our day on Sea Spray and with confidence boosted I talked to Kim, only to find similar (although I found out much later, not as strong) thoughts on his mind. We chose a sunny day and headed out to Blue Water Marina for the first time. For some reason the site office was shut but we parked our car and walked around the marina. The sun glittered on the water, everywhere was peace, boaters were friendly and chatty, some working on their boats, some sitting in the sun. It felt right to me and I wondered if we would ever be lucky enough to call this home. I so badly wanted to be part of it all. We went home fired with enthusiasm and being me, I decided before we looked at any specific boats we needed to know what we were looking at. There is a wealth of information on any subject on the worldwide web and narrow boats are no exception. This started a pattern that continues to this day – you can look anything up!

My job for an IT firm meant I was almost a professional at Googling info and a few clicks took me to the excellent Canal and River Trust website and their "handy guide" A boat of your own, for everyone new to boat ownership. This covered almost everything as well as giving links to independent sites written by "boaters" to help newcomers. I also found websites written by people already living on narrow boats itemising the costs, monthly, quarterly and annual and I spent hours working out our living costs and making copious lists to help us in our decision making trying to ensure we were as knowledgeable as possible – very comforting things lists!

We have had an 'interesting' life preferring to try things rather than sit in a nine to five existence. A corner shop in Somerset (our first experience of selling up for a new life), a social club on the Somerset Dorset border and then a company relocation with my job in wine to deepest Yorkshire meant our mortgage still had years to run. I would need to work till my mid seventies at least and I suddenly began to realise I was working a forty to fifty hour week for an IT company, admittedly from home, on the phone all day to support a lifestyle I no longer enjoyed or wanted. Our three children were settled with partners and families of their own and although we were always there for them they didn't need day to day support anymore. Also I love being outside and spent hours on a seat in the garden of our little white cottage down a lane in a Yorkshire village. As summer turned to autumn and Yorkshire evenings got colder I was still loath to go inside and with a battered leather hat on my head, much to the amusement of the locals – Kim used to call me the 'White Witch of Camblesforth' – took to wrapping a large red plaid blanket around me determined not to go inside even when my fingers turned white on the pages of my book. I resented the winter more and more and my enforced time shut up inside, cut off from the weather and the fresh air, the sun in winter and the silence at twilight. In a house you miss so much. Putting this together with my financial calculations I worked out that selling up, paying off our mortgage and debts meant living a lovely life completely debt free. It all sounded so easy!

Over the next few months we remained firm in our decision whilst coming up with any excuse not to act on it. "Let's wait till after our winter break", "Let's get my birthday out the way", "No one does anything just before Christmas!" It was the end of December when I saw the advert in the local press offering to sell your property for 1% if you gave them a sole agency in the first week of January. In a brave moment I rang and made an appointment, then spent the rest of the day panicking about it, telling myself I could still back out. When I told Kim he agreed that it was a good idea but with a stunned look that said, 'we are actually going to do this?' I continued looking up narrow boats on line after meeting with a lovely estate agent – a middle-aged woman who had recently set up her own business; she was very good and fell in love with our tiny and quirky cottage. I had seen other agents who had said variously, "it isn't everyone's cup of tea", "we may find it difficult" and "we'll need to mark it down if you want to sell it!" After showing a few couples around I was thoroughly disheartened. One couple had loved it, but found it far too small, one woman wanted to buy it but didn't have the funds – a friend would lend her the balance, she was sure! A lovely gay couple came and said it was ideal except there was no dining room for dinner parties and the bedroom too small for what they had it mind. Finally a young woman came with her mother, in her early twenties and married to a serving solider; she was looking for their first home and fell absolutely in love with our cottage! There would no problems as they had their finances sorted including a deposit from the army. I did love the cottage and wanted to sell it to someone who felt the same. It was March by then and we agreed on a sale, I told them that if we got the asking price we would leave most of the furniture as none of it would fit on a narrow boat, they agreed.

I can remember looking around at our belongings, all the furniture we had accumulated over thirty five years of marriage and each piece full of memories. Certain pieces still tug at me – the dressing table in an antique shop I fell in love with over twenty years ago that my late father then went back and secretly bought for me. The Welsh pine dresser bought in our first years together that had aged with our marriage. Neither would fit on a narrow boat, I did not want to lose either of them, but if we were going to do this….

My books were another matter. To say I love reading is an understatement; I have spent my life reading, as a child instead of getting ready for school. As a teenager told to 'watch the grill' I sat there engrossed whilst it caught fire, and as an adult it has caused much exasperation on the part of my husband as I completely ignore him, buried as I am in a book.

As well as buying and acquiring my favourites I have done book reviews for a local newspaper keeping the books afterwards. In fact I have kept all my books and cannot understand people who don't. This has left me with several bookcases full of books and plastic boxes crammed full stored under the bed. I knew I had to get rid of them, I knew this, but was doing a wonderful example of an ostrich until Kim said, if I didn't sort most of them out he would have to dump the lot. It took several attempts and many arguments as I ran down the lane to our garage and emptied the bag from the van before it left for the charity shops, convinced I could not live without a particular book. Finally I got it down to about fifty books (it has already grown to seventy) agreeing that more would certainly sink us!

Kim could very easily become a minimalist apart from a few items he cannot part with; his pair of Zulu assegais', his Victorian constables truncheon, his 1850 percussion cap rifle and most importantly some books that were definitely coming with us – the series of fantasy novels it has taken him 11yrs to complete that are based on the lives and adventures of some fresh water fish. 'The Broadwaters Trilogy' has seen him compared to Henry Williamson in an Amazon review. They were taking pride of place when we commenced life aboard.

I am a hoarder, wrapping my belongings around me in my tiny home. He therefore took to this easily disposing of items with scarcely a thought whilst I performed a sort of tug-of-war with myself, never mind him, knowing items had to go whilst desperately hanging on to them. The couple buying our property were keen to move quickly, we had met the husband and he loved the cottage as much as she did. Everything moved quickly except for the army. The deposit we were told was on its way, it turned out to be 'on its way' for nearly six months as it was September before we moved.

During this time we had been making numerous visits to various boat yards and marinas. We had viewed several boats and finally knew what we could afford and what facilities we required. From my point of view my number one priority was a permanent double bed as I wasn't going to be making a bed every night! After that cupboard space, a bath/shower, cooker and fridge and enough room bow and stern to be able to sit out in the summer months. My favourite (and easily affordable) marina was called Blue Water in Thorne, South Yorkshire being just out of town and beautifully peaceful, also if we bought a boat from them we would automatically get a permanent mooring there, something that can sometimes prove elusive. This enabled us to come down to a short list of three boats:-

Yorkshireman.

Traditional end...Side of bed folds over – bed's legs in the air? Fridge, cooker, table, radiator...blind in kitchen, arm chairs, wall lights, wood burner, two sets of bookshelves purple tiles in bathroom, port holes in bedroom, phone at aft/intercom, glass cupboard between kitchen area and lounge above gap.

Northern Star.

Wood floors, bookcase, large wood burner, integral cooker and fridge, no bath just a shower, bed out permanently, port holes in bedroom.

Bodhran.

Cruiser end, bed out permanently, space above bed – drawer for books? Flat cupboards, along side of boat, bathroom with bath, heated towel rail and shower. Pretty shelf unit in kitchen area, cooker (brand new), fridge, several cupboards, hot water heater, wood burner, custom made awning covers bow and stern though cannot stand up completely at bow end.

Bodhran...... second viewing and the details required:

Engine hours...20833, built 2000, by David Clarke, 45ft Excluding fenders, Beam 6ft 10inch...Draft Swim, 20 inches, water line aft 23 inches. British Safety Certificate till 24th 04 2018. Vetus Engine, 30 hp. 30.4.14. Pennine Cruisers Skipton pressure wash, anodes, flexible fuel hoses and cable ties supplied and fit weed hatch, two leisure batteries. Hull report with ultra sonic testing..25/4/14...structure and integrity, very good and showing no significant deterioration.

They all had their pluses and minuses and we liked all three boats but gradually we found ourselves mainly considering Bodhran. She was in good condition throughout and I thought her very cosy. With tongue and groove woodwork in the main, and good sized fridge, new cooker, plenty of kitchen units, shower and hip-bath and a fixed double bed, I could definitely see us living there. More practically she had two new leisure batteries, a new water pump and new awnings to bow and stern. Initially, in my innocence I was not sure about her due to the awnings until it was pointed out that they were easily removable in the summer, worth around £2k as they were fully customised and in winter were invaluable, as they have proved to be for storage, coats, shoes, boots, fuel, wood etc.etc. Finally – and this really swayed it for us – she had had a hull survey completed four months previously and been 'blacked' and had new anodes fitted at the same time. Her boat safety certificate would last

another three and a half years. This would save us around £1k in surveys and for our first boat we would be sure all of this had been attended to giving us time to learn about our new way of life! We made our decision and let 'Blue Water' know that we intended buying Bodhran subject to being taken out on her. We were told that they would let the present owner know but that nothing could be binding until a deposit was made. We explained about the army and the deposit being 'on its way' and promised to chase up the solicitor.

It was a couple of weeks later following several promises of 'we will exchange on the house any day now' when I received a phone call from Sarah at Blue Water explaining that someone wanted to put a deposit down on Bodhran. She knew how keen we were but she could not hold him off forever. I took a deep breath and found myself giving a firm promise to buy Bodhran and send a deposit that very day. When I put the phone down I felt sick. I had just promised to buy a boat for around £35k that I didn't have as we hadn't exchanged yet. I didn't even have the deposit until then. I knew we were due to exchange but I couldn't help thinking of the time we sold our grocers shop (Highburn General Stores) in Somerset. After weeks of negotiation and on the day of exchange I had phoned our prospective buyers to ask if they had heard anything yet only to be told they had pulled out. They told me they didn't have the money they said they had and had thought 'something' would turn up! I phoned our solicitors assistant in a panic and explained about Bodhran. Our solicitor was lovely, if a bit vague, but his assistant was very organized and knew we had been waiting to exchange for a while "we're going to have to get this moving for you straight away". I was upstairs in my office and called Kim; he was very calm saying we would just have to wait and see and disappeared. I did not find this particularly helpful as I was not calm and paced, heart thumping until I finally received a call from our solicitor to say it had all gone through and he was paying our deposit on Bodhran. I phoned the marina to let Sarah know full details re the deposit, sat down and still felt sick. This was it. There was no going back! My mother's voice kept floating across to me "you may like boats but that doesn't mean you go to live on one. You just don't!"

I'd like to say that I remember the rest of that day but I don't except for a propensity to frantically make list after list of what we needed to do, to buy, to finish and to get rid of. I then probably sat down with a book and some wine! I do know that the following day we went to see Bodhran, this time in the knowledge that she would soon be all ours. It felt so good; I loved her and knew it was the right decision. It was a lovely evening, dusk was falling with a beautiful sunset and I could see us sitting out in the evening enjoying the peace and quiet. This was the life I wanted!

We had two weeks to either clear or pack our belongings. Most of the furniture was staying and we had a car boot sale and cleared a lot of our possessions making £147! One thing I can say is that I have not missed any of them. Getting rid of most of the things you own is very cathartic, even for a hoarder like me, and I have felt a lot freer since. Finally the day of departure came. As always it was manic and exhausting, but we were determined to clean and polish everything giving the cottages new owners a clean home to start with. It was strange leaving knowing we would never return there, but my spirits rose when we arrived at the marina. Living here is very peaceful. On board you are rarely interrupted or disturbed by anyone, however activities outside the boat are fair game and likely to gain an audience – move in on a warm day and they all want to see how you get on. There is a real sense of community here so it is good natured and if you have a problem they will all lend a hand, they may take the mickey at the same time but they will always help! We set to and emptied our boxes and bags from the car and van onto the boat. We then attempted to unpack and unfortunately realised that Kim had been right! We still had too much, something he made sure I knew, as did our audience. Much to their amusement we then removed the bags and boxes from the boat to the canal bank outside, luckily it wasn't raining. We unpacked and started sorting them out again, putting a lot back into the van. We were definitely coming at this from different angles! Kim was looking at each item and saying 'Is it necessary' 'does it perform a useful function' Mr. Spock could not have been more logical. I on the other hand needed several items to make the boat look like home, create a cosy atmosphere and be warm and welcoming. Frustrated he became even more limited and logical in what he felt was right as I happily decided on pictures, ornaments, throws, crystals and of course, most essential, books! Since then certain items have found their way back on board after being banned, not to mention the autumn garlands I put up in October!

We were shattered! We did enough to enable us to have a comfy evening and first night. I made up the bed and we then repaired to the foredeck, removing the awning to sit in the evening sun with a beer and a glass of wine facing out into the water. We had done it. All those months of waiting and we were here. There was very little sound other than birdsong and the odd quack from a passing duck. A light breeze sprung up and a pink and gold tinge edged the clouds as evening drew near. Making dinner in the galley kitchen with the bow doors open to the outside world was wonderful, a completely different world and I loved it.

We had arrived! Arguing over which possessions were joining us we had packed, unpacked, repacked, fought and put most of our belongings back in the van! The only item of furniture joining us from the cottage was the coffee table with the top made from a single and unusual piece of wood that Kim had saved from a skip years ago when we were first married. It was a welcome and familiar face. On our first evening we sat on two wooden

41

folding chairs completely exhausted and made a list of everything we needed; sofa or armchairs, throw, TV, aerial, rug, and side lamps. Much to Kim's horror I suggested a certain flat pack department store and he reluctantly agreed. We had the children and their families coming over in a couple of days and I was determined to be ready. I had decided on my colour scheme with a dark sofa, black or grey, with bright red accessories (think Danish Hygge) that I thought would coordinate well with the golden tones of the wood and give the cosy atmosphere I so wanted. The following day we headed for the treadmill that is shopping at this particular place with very specific measurements. For a narrow boat furniture must not only fit snugly into place leaving enough room for movement but must also fit through the vessels doors. An exhausting few hours later we had everything we needed for the interior of the boat and I was pleased with the result. A phone call from our son Martyn saying he and his family would like to call in the following day and see us gave us our first boat argument! Kim was insistent we would not all fit in and we would have to go to a restaurant or pub I was just as insistent that this was our home now and we would welcome them here and feed them here! It was a beautiful hot and sunny September day and Kim finally said it was a shame we didn't have a table and bench set on our little grassy area outside the boat. Cue for an instant trip into Doncaster where we completely unable to find anything to suit. That evening I frantically trawled the internet and found one not far from our old cottage at a garden centre we visited early next day. I was sorting food and drink and keeping an eye out for them and Kim was still putting the bench set together when they arrived. I loved showing them around, so proud of our new home. Charlie our 8 year old grandson was fascinated by it all and by having grandparents that actually lived on a boat! We promised him he could come and stay and have a day out, fishing included. After that the rest of the family took it in turns to visit and view Bodhran. Our other son Mark and his wife came to lunch, and daughter Jessica and her family came as well. Her children Evie and Oliver 4 and 2 were amazed that anyone lived on a boat! We had Oliver's 2nd birthday party on our new bench set and I loved Evie's first comment……. "Grandma!! it's got a bed in it!!! " …..said in complete amazement.

Living aboard a Narrow Boat. (At moorings)

Where do I begin? Let's start with the basics - We have in Bodhran a toilet cassette system, there are of course other means of disposing of unwanted matter from your boat, such as pump out (no description needed there surely!) but we felt that this method was more to our liking. The cassette slides into its compartment at the base of the toilet and you empty the contents into the sluice (at your moorings or at specific points along the canal) when necessary...it is that simple. There are on the market certain liquid or dry chemicals that do a great job in dissolving solid material and masking odours. Whilst the boat is at its moorings we tend to use the marinas facilities as much as possible but on cruising of course the cassette is vital...not to mention extremely *convenient and relieving*.

During periods of mooring we are connected to the mains electric by way of a four way (feeding other boats alongside us) distribution post, this power is governed through the site office and we pay for our electric usage through them. Our boat has two leisure batteries that are trickle fed by an on/off charger and kept charged for use when we are cruising. We have a 250 volt inverter aboard but the main lights, water pump and fridge are all 12 volts and run by the batteries. We have a gas supply by way of an independent cylinder and we fill our 620 litre integral water tank by hose from a communal water standpipe. We have T.V. Wi-Fi a shower and diesel run heaters if required…we never have, our little coal and wood burning, eco fan assisted burner gives us all the heat we require and some! So you see, we have all the mod cons you could wish for! In the summer we have the birdsong in the winter the moon and stars….what more could you possibly need?

At points along the canal towpaths and clearly marked in the various waterways charts and maps are fresh water standpipes, these can be used for filling personal water containers and of course your boats own tanks. Bodhran's large fresh water tank is filled by means of a hose pipe connected to the standpipe fed directly into a water aperture in the bow. It takes about an hour to replenish our boat so good time to read the newspaper over nice cup of tea and a couple of biscuits whilst waiting.

Bodhrans engine is a Vetus 30 hp diesel and it was initially housed under a considerably heavy, solid steel cratch plate recessed into the sterns deck. To access the weed box, batteries and engine compartment you had to take your life in your hands and lever the said plate up, tilt it and prop it up precariously using a piece of four x four. Having a fondness for all my fingers and toes I had to do something about this situation as the cratch plate would easily double up as a guillotine if I were not ultra careful. After several attempts at fitting a securing chain or a more solid type of fixing prop I soon realised that not only was the plate too heavy, when raised it used up valuable room on the stern deck and made getting into the engine compartment a job for Twizzle (for those of you old enough to remember him!!!). Here we get to illustrating the wonderful (we can help) attitude that abounds amongst boaters. After a while a small group of them had appeared on the tow path watching (with a certain amount of undisguised amusement I may add) my unsuccessful attempts to rectify my 'heavy' problem…… In the wink of an eye an angle grinder had appeared and soon the large single solid cratch plate was cut in half making two much lighter smaller cratch plates that would prove to be much safer and far easier to use. I now have all my fingers and toes and a few more friends into the bargain.

Learning all the time.

The first time it happened was just two days before New Year's Eve, we decided that it was a one-off fault with the electricity distribution post or too many appliances were being used at once in our neighbouring boats. It was late at night and Bodhrans lights were dimming and the red light on the little fridge flashing red. I switched on the 250 volt inverter and it sounded an alarm…I would investigate fully tomorrow. During the following day all was ok with the world the lights were back to bright but the fridge still flashed intermittently…later on when the need came for the boats lights to be put on they dimmed again and we found the water pump did not work to its full potential…. 'Houston we have a problem'…..Having

checked the voltage from the leisure batteries with my newly purchased volt meter...and getting a good 12 volts from each I realised the culprit could only be the little red box situated under our bed...the trickle charger. Where to get a new charger? Which type did I need? How much would it cost? Where would be the best place to get it? As I pondered all these questions sitting on what Linda and I call our "poop deck" a familiar voice sounded from the bank..."What's up our kid you look troubled?"...
"Looks like my chargers on the blink, where do you think I can get a new one at this time of day?"...... "Hold yer 'orses" came the reply and the voice and its owner walked back towards their own boat moored a few hundred feet from ours. Within an hour I had the 'borrow this until you can get a new one" charger fitted and Bodhran was lit up like a Christmas tree.....yet another example of the wonderful camaraderie that is rife amongst boat people.

Knots

He was standing on the grass at Bodhrans stern and he had two loops of the stuff over each arm, made of nylon, pale green with yellow, red and blue strands, each 30 metres in length.

"Do you want to buy new mooring ropes mate - I've been clearing out my shed - only a fiver?"

How could I resist? Our existing ropes were too thick, too dirty, too old and far too long. I never quite got round to shortening them, once undone from the moorings and laid over the roof and decks they fell in wide coils and created too much of a tripping hazard!...at a fiver each he was *'literally giving these new ones away'* I bought a length.

I had more than enough of the nylon rope for bow, midship and stern, it took me no time at all to cut the old ones free and throw them away leaving just one length tied to prevent 'Bodders' from going for a sail up the canal all on her own. Once I had cut the required lengths of the new ropes I sealed the ends by offering them up to a lighted candle and melting the strands together to form blackened stumps which I taped over, this prevents fraying and strand seperation. I was finally ready to attach the ropes to the boat ….and I did, 'in a fashion'

"You can't tie her up like that, it looks so, so untidy" It was Linda sitting on our bench looking up from her book…"It just doesn't look neat, it looks like a 'lump of tangled spaghetti' there are proper knots you know….I've seen them in our 'Boaters Guide'

I left her with her book and frown and went down into the galley to get the 'guide'…I have to admit the precise art of knot tying was an essential boaters skill that neither of us had paid adequate attention to…it was high time we mastered it.

I placed the book (opened to the appropriate page) on Bodhrans roof, lay the end of the rope alongside a diagram of a knot and procceded to copy it. I chose the Bowline.

No matter how many times I tried I could not get to it do what it was supposed to do. When I took it to the boats mooring hook put it over and pulled it tight– I succeeded in making it look like...'a lump of tangled spaghetti'!

 Linda then stepped up, attempted it once and got it right first time, it was obvious to me she'd simply been watching where I'd gone wrong .....I'd made it easy for her her!

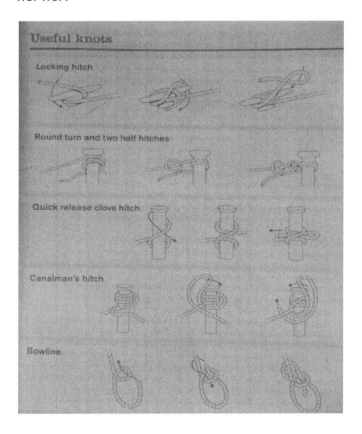

His name was Richard and he charged us £50 for 4hrs tuition navigating our boat, money well spent. We'd been out on our own of course many times on Devon but she was smaller than Bodhran by 20 feet and the marina we were in had little room for manoeuvre (the entrance also being the exit was tight and the angle from the moorings themselves acute) catching out many a seasoned boater. Once out of the marina and onto the wide Stainforth and Keadby Canal it was, excuse the pun, plain sailing and my prowess at steering a steady course soon came back to me. Richard pointed out a few obvious safety tips such as the wearing of life jackets, especially when negotiating locks and weirs, to watch out for tripping hazards such as mooring ropes, bollards and holes. He advised the wearing of non slip shoes, keeping all ropes dry and neatly curled, resisting the temptation of jumping from boat to bank and keeping the roof of the vessel clear of all unnecessary articles. Our mooring ropes were too long, they needed shortening and placed so they could be easily reached from either side of the boat, my fishing tackle tied together and left stashed under the skirt of the awning was *in the way*, and the new T.V. aerial I'd fitted on the hand rail would be fine for receiving 200 + channels but entirely useless at hanging onto if I did manage to trip on its (dangling over the edge) wiring!!

Aim your stick at it to miss it… This simple instruction imparted by Richard to us both was probably the one that helped most in the day to day navigation of Bodhran and will be of use to all novice skippers. If you are confronted with an object ahead on the canal, albeit another boat coming towards you, or the jutting out wall/ bollard of a weir or lock, hold your tiller and point the end of it (stern or starboard) directly at it...and immediately your bow will be directed away....easy!

The Kitchen

The galley kitchen consists of two sets of units facing each other, one five foot long made up of two base cupboards and a fridge under a worktop, the other seven foot long made up of a sink drainer unit with cupboards underneath, a gas cooker and a single base cupboard. There is a two foot wide space between. In terms of cupboard space I manage very easily as I had very little space in the cottage, but it took a while to adjust to the closeness of the units whilst cooking. I liken it to the 'dance' described by workers behind the bar as they moved round each other and I took some time finding my own 'dance'. For instance you can only have one door open at a time. You cannot look in the fridge if a cupboard door is open and you cannot open a cupboard door if you are using the grill etc.etc... also, the lack of worktop space means you cannot get everything out prior to cooking a meal – not and manage to prepare veg.etc at the same time. We love a Sunday dinner, old fashioned maybe, but I enjoy the whole process. After the first one on the boat I was ready to give up! I twisted and turned, bumping into every door and cupboard, nearly dropped the meat laden meat dish getting the joint out of the oven, never mind trying to sort out a space on the cooker top to make the gravy. Even now I have to be careful taking anything out of the oven (I have to stand sideways to the cooker) making sure the lack of space doesn't mean I catch the edge of the dish on the cooker and upend everything on the floor! As I said, I managed easily putting everything away as the cupboards are quite deep. The first time I needed an ingredient or two for a sauce I reached in, knocked a couple of bottles over and everything collapsed in a domino effect into a total mess! After this happened a couple of times in complete frustration I had a light bulb moment, took myself to a local store and bought a lot of small plastic trays, problem solved. All the small ingredients; stock, garlic paste, corn flour, pesto etc. fit into these trays and lifting one out even if I have to get to the 'seldom used' tray at the back is much easier. Very few modern kitchens nowadays have armchairs in them. One thing I love is the fact is that on Bodhran my chair is right next to the galley and the view outside is wonderful. Sitting reading or knitting whilst something savoury simmers on the stove, the ducks and swans go floating past and I have a lovely view of sky and trees always reminds me why I did this in the first place.

The Bedroom

There are many things that can be more difficult when living on a narrow boat as opposed to a house. There is a'physicality' about the life that I actually enjoy, apart from the horror of making a double bed! Our bed is set in an alcove and is completely surrounded on three sides. It is far higher than a normal bed in a house, the top of the bed being 2ft 6ins off the floor, this makes climbing on and off the bed strangely reminiscent of childhood, especially if you are as short as I am. In order to make the bed and tuck in the sheets you have to physically lift the mattress with one hand whilst – due to the height – being bent double over the open side and quickly whip the sheets under the mattress, hanging on at the corner when you drop the said mattress. The duvet also needs to be tucked in along the wall side otherwise one person gets all the bedding! This I found was best accomplished by clambering on top if the bed and shoving the duvet down the side. Once made up I was very pleased, I topped the bed with a throw we bought in Canada from folk artist Lucy Ogletree. It shows the four seasons and I love it. It gives just the right feeling for the boat and really comes into its own. So we were set for our first sleep 'onboard'.

Something I had not considered is that a narrow boat bed can be smaller than a standard double bed, a three quarter bed size I think. We tried to settle down. I had insisted on sleeping on the same side as we always had, this meant me on the outside and Kim on the inside sleeping face to face with the side of the boat. We just weren't used to such a lack of space having previously slept in a king sized bed! Bums, knees and elbows were bumping and scraping against each other as we attempted to reach our usual sleeping positions. After a few nights Kim came up with a calm and perfectly reasoned argument as to why we should sleep the other way round i.e. with our heads where our feet were now. Naturally, he agreed with me that we should keep to the sides we had always slept on – he knew I wanted that. So – this meant I would be on the inside and he on the outside. The end of his argument was actually tinged with a touch of desperation! It somehow made sense and I do think the bed makes more sense this way round. As well, I am extremely short sighted so at night it does not trouble me to sleep about four inches away from a wall. I couldn't see it anyway. We have also adjusted to the space and have found new sleeping positions that involve sleeping with all limbs in a straight line! The final word on changing the bed? Changing the sheets is an exhausting process, changing the duvet cover in a very limited space means you have to be creative. A fellow 'liveaboard '* told me that in good weather it is easier to change the cover on the canal bank as you simply can't shake a duvet into its cover on a narrow boat. There is no room!

*Liveaboards are as the name suggests...they live aboard...and then we get ' boaters' and 'floaters'....boaters live on board and cruise the canals frequently...'floaters' live aboard and are happy to remained moored up all year round.

Everyday Life

Every day life began to fall into place, although there are some 'firsts' that can be mentioned such as emptying the loo! We were using the toilet on the marina in the early mornings and I have seen some beautiful mornings strolling down. In summer when the air is fresh and everything still and quiet. Ducks, swans and geese are employed at various places preening themselves and although they will cautiously study you as you walk past they generally ignore you. The sun is out, glittering on the water, birds are singing in the trees on their dawn chorus and all is peaceful. I also love the winter mornings, with ice everywhere and a delicious freshness in the air. The sun is winterbright, the air fresh with an exhilarating bite. I even like the cold and windy mornings, with trees rustling and twisting and I bundle up warm with heavy boots on for my morning constitutional. On this particular day however for the first time our cassette toilet was full!

I was a little disconcerted by the whole 'emptying the loo' scenario. Since my childhood abroad and the many summers spent travelling around Italy, toilets in England deal with all of that! One flush and it disappears. Emptying a toilet with its week of 'waste' and I didn't have a clue. We had been using the recommended blue fluid – called Blue – in the cassette and so far had had no problems. Today, trying to look as if we knew what we were doing we got the sack truck, staggered outside with the very heavy cassette and headed for the sluice. The sluice actually looks like an oversized toilet set in a sink unit with a cistern and chain above. I had studied (really!) how to empty a cassette toilet from the many videos loaded onto Youtube. As directed I found the small door on the boat set in the wall at the back of the toilet, I knew how to remove the cassette and on reaching the sluice I knew to press the button on the top of the cassette to let in air before upending the whole thing to empty it out. It was actually very easy! Using "Blue" combined with our early morning walks to the facilities and we were done in no time. We walked back to the boat with a clean and very much lighter cassette, loaded it back in and forgot about it for another week. What had seemed to be an onerous task soon became a normal and every day part of life. The other main alternative on a narrow boat is a tank integral to the body of the vessel. When this is full you attend a pumping out station and the whole thing is emptied by suction. It never appealed to us.

Day to day life aboard a narrow boat can be more physical but that is something I actively enjoy. We have the obligatory water tank on board and as well as the standard taps we have a filter tap attached to the kitchen sink. The water is very clean but can become stale especially as the water level drops and we decided to buy a large plastic container from a camping shop and fill that regularly from the standpipe on the marina to use for drinking water. I quite enjoy my walks outside to fill it.

I was never a tidy 'skirt and heels' type of dresser. My preferred mode of dress being kaftan and jeans but life on board positively encourages casual dress. One of the advantages for me is the free and easy way of life. A boat day spent at home doing chores and pottering about and I am very content. As I sit here writing this on our bench set outside Bodhran, it is a lovely sunny day. Gold /Brown Kaftan, sandals, a cup of tea or glass of wine and lots of birdsong and I am in heaven.

Today there is a lot of talk about your ecological footprint. I think that living on a narrow boat makes you more aware of the natural resources you use and certainly more environmentally conscious. I never leave taps running whilst washing and certainly never fill up a bowl when washing up! You get used to being prepared and not taking anything for granted. Before making

dinner and settling in for the night I like to make sure that I have enough water for the evening meal and for tea in the morning. I keep a weather eye on the toilet level and listen for the change in the noise the water pump makes showing the water level is getting low.

Our bathroom, whilst fully functional does not exactly encourage you to waste water. It has a hip bath with shower over, a sink with a large cupboard underneath, a toilet, small medicine cabinet and two metal shelves. It is small, definitely very small and at first with dark wood and the carpeting on the walls so beloved of narrow boats, a dark green shade it seemed gloomy and pokey to say the least. Certainly not a luxurious, loll about for hours, type of bathroom! On my first morning I got up, turned on the electricity (we turn it off at night) and went in to wash as usual. The bathroom although clean seemed minute and I made it one of my tasks on our first day on Bodhran to scrub it thoroughly top to bottom. The shower is good, but is not a power shower by any means. Kim prefers to save our water and walk down to use the marina shower. He has more room, a more powerful shower and does not leave our bathroom looking a complete mess! I soon adjusted to the size of the room and now love to use the bath. At night with only a small port hole shaded to give privacy it so warm and cosy by candle light. Being in the bath in the flickering light when the rain is drumming on the roof and the boat is gently rocking really cannot be beaten. We have since brightened the bathroom up by painting the wood a pale cream, and buying some new cream flooring and it has lifted the whole room.

Our First Solo Trip In Bodhran (Bodders)

It was a pleasant Friday morning in August 2015. The weather was perfect, very little breeze, warm and sunny. Of course we'd taken 'Bodders' out before with Richard and gained a lot of experience on narrow boat Devon and on Dave and Annette's 23ft cruiser Sea Spray but this was different, daunting, awesome and frankly - terrifying. On board our boat apart from us, was our home, our belongings, our lives...over dramatising things I hear you say?....well maybe, but all the same Linda and I were full of trepidation, not helped of course by the crowd of well wishers lining the marina's banks (a boat leaving the marina turns everybody into meerkats, necks stretching high, eyes squinting against the suns reflection on the waters) Who's that going out?

It's Kim and Linda on Bodhran.

Navigating out of the marina requires a certain amount of concentration as the angles are tight and it is embarrassing if you 'bump' another boat. It takes a while to get used to the fact that to go right the tiller needs to be pushed to the left and vice versa (and be patient as the vessel takes a few seconds to respond) also narrow boats do not steer in reverse (unless fitted with 'bow thrusters) so to go backwards you need to steer forward the way you intend to go back and then put your engine into reverse.. another point to consider is the boat pivots from its centre, so in turning you have to aim to turn halfway along its length...to add to all of this try and remember what I have failed to remember on several occasions...you cannot steer a boat without the engine in gear...*no gear, no steer.*

We had planned our *'maiden voyage'* in some detail the night before and although it took in only four locks**, a number of road bridges* and a stop at a local pub (essential) it would take over 36 hrs allowing for an overnight stop...*there is no rushing on any canal.* We would be cruising at a leisurely 4 knots from South End, Thorne along the Stainforth and Keadby canal to the New Junction Canal at Bramwith turning back near the Don Aqueduct for our return home, an intrepid, if short journey indeed.

A Typical Lock.

If you follow a series of step–by–step procedures using locks will become second nature to you as we have found. Locks are simply chambers with gates at either end. Emptying or filling the chamber enables you to move your boat up or down onto a new section of the waterway. There are many different types of locks but they all work on the same principle. Once the gates are closed you can open the sluices or paddles to let the water in or out. When the water level under your boat is the same as the level you're moving toward you'll be able to open the gates to move in or out of the lock. If you are sharing the lock with another boat all well and good your work should be shared and normally is!

Some locks are operated by the user others have designated lock-keepers; this information will be made available to you on the lock instructions and local information.

We have found by experience that in wide or river locks it's better to keep your boat 'steady' by using your bow and stern ropes looped around the bollards. In narrow locks we tend to use the boats engine to control her (keeping well away from the cill) and always close the gates when leaving a lock unless there is a boat coming towards us.

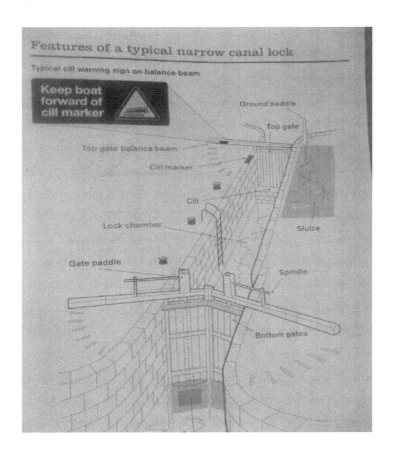

Features of a typical narrow canal lock

Typical cill warning sign on balance beam

Keep boat
forward of
cill marker

Ground paddle

Top gate

Top gate balance beam

Cill marker

Cill

Lock chamber

Sluice

Gate paddle

Spindle

Bottom gates

A Typical Mechanised Road Bridge.

A Guillotine Lock.

A Swivel road bridge.

Common signs.

First things first, the disconnection from our land supply of electricity, I have heard many tales of this being accidently overlooked and it can prove to be costly, the male and female couplings are heavy duty all weather-proof fittings and have a metal clip holding them together, they don't take kindly to being tugged haphazardly from the supply posts. I disconnect 'Bodders' and store the cable safely in its home in a compartment in the bow. We are now dependant on our two leisure batteries for electric power in the boat. The tiller rod (which is usually solid brass and hugely desirable to any passing magpie) is taken from its storage place in the boat and fitted to the tiller itself. The midship ropes are then untied from the pontoon and laid in a tidy manner so that they can be reached from either starboard or port side and do not present a tripping hazard. We have already cleared the roof of all unnecessary items (you can tell a liveaboard by all the storage on top of the boat!) all that remains are the boat hook, gang plank, barge pole and a life buoy. A quick check to make sure all our fenders are in place and we are ready to untie the ropes at 'Bodder's' stern, store them neatly aboard, start the 30 horse power engine and gently slip her into gear.

With the satisfying chug, chug of the engine thrumming below our feet we are off, no two departures are ever the same and the feeling of total freedom I get from them never diminishes.

Out from the relative shelter of our moorings and safely away from the boats either side of us, I push the tiller hard to the left and 'Bodder's' bow drifts to the right until we are in the centre of the marina, I do the opposite once we are at the marina's mouth, sound the horn to warn others that may be passing and we are finally in the open waters of the Stainforth and Keadby canal, heading at a sedate speed towards Doncaster. Along the banks the fishermen eye us with a mixture of annoyance and resignation, we smile sweetly, thank them if they have to bring their lines in and are all the time aware of our speed and the size of bow wave – it is never our intention to disturb their peace and we always do our utmost not to but we need to pass!

Out in the open, in the centre of the canal and away from other moored boats we give 'Bodders' near her full throttle, we are now travelling at the huge speed of 4 knots with the wind in our hair (what I've got left of mine) and in no hurry to go any faster. Arriving at the destination, any destination, is not the aim of the narrow boat, if you want to get somewhere, go by train, car, or bus, if you want to 'see' where you are going to 'hear' where you are going, to 'smell 'where you are going, to 'taste' where you are going……go by narrow boat!

"Put the kettle on first mate", "Aye aye Skipper"….we hadn't gone more than a mile and our first lock/bridge was upon us. I'd slowed 'Bodders' into the bank moored up and secured her to the landing stage bollards. We were in no hurry, there wasn't another boat in sight, we were holding nobody back but ourselves and the thought of a nice cup of tea amongst the inquisitive swans and ducks was more than appealing. With the boats engine off the sudden and almost complete silence was glorious, apart from the gentle lapping of water against hull and continuous birdsong the world was at peace. Two mugs of steaming tea appeared from the relative darkness of the galley as if by magic and the scene was set...On the stern we leant side by side against the taff rail hands cupped around our hot beverages "I'll wager ya spiced this 'ere grog wi a tot or two o' rum ya scurvy knave" Linda stared back at me an incredulous look on her face and said nothing. I don't think the 'scurvy knave' bit went down too well!

It was time for the off and a few more unhurried bends, straights and a couple of locks in the canal before we reached our moorings for the night. We'd chosen a remote part of the canal but within walking distance of a public house (references to public houses in this book will not be infrequent) ....an evening meal chased down with a nice wine and we'd be set for the night.

And what a night! ...with the canopies down aft and stern our ceiling now a blanket of pitch black lit up with pin pricks of brilliant light from a trillion stars, our table lamp the alabaster white of a full moon and the only sounds that of a stillness in the air that holds everything its captive. We are alone in the universe and at nobody's calling.

The morning and another sunny day, after a leisurely breakfast we would head up canal a mile or so to our turning point, do a wide 'u' turn and point our bow to home. The return journey would be as unhurried as the outward one, our only aim...to be moored up before nightfall and there would be plenty of time for that.

A short foray indeed but as with all canal journeys a highly enjoyable one.

I have always loved fishing; not only writing about it but doing it - see my trilogy of books, (The Broadwater Trilogy). Although, I hasten to add the said books are not wholly about the physicality of fishing but more about the fish themselves and the lives I fantasize they lead below the water's surface. When my boat chores are done, the weather suitable and I have a few hours to spare I like nothing more than sitting at 'Bodders' stern and doing a spot of fishing. The fish in the marina are mainly small fry, namely, perch, dace, bleak, roach and the occasional bream but there are of course (no doubt due to the small fry being in such abundance) the insatiable and highly successful predators, pike.

The pike play a major role in all three of my books, being the villains of the piece, the aggressors, the merciless murderers lurking deep in the shadows beneath the hull of the narrow boats ready to strike at......but wait a minute, that is all for you to read in my books..the bit I'm about to tell you is true, not fantasy...it really happened and my dear wife Linda was there to witness it all.

I'd been fishing for about an hour using very light tackle and bits of rolled up bread catching the occasional small perch and I was quite happy with my 'lot'. Fishing for me is the best way to meditate and totally relax, I'd just drifted off on yet another reverie.....when I had another bite, my float disappeared from view and I could immediately feel the gentle tug of a moderately sized fish on the hook. I stood up from my little boaters chair and made to reel it in. Linda was sitting on our bench reading her book and was, as she always is when reading, completely absorbed. As my reel quickly gathered my line in the small fish came towards me its futile wriggling sending darts of silver flashing through the murky waters. And then I saw it, less than two metres from the bank and zeroing in on my little fish at a terrifying speed….the unmistakable shape of a pike! From then on everything happened in a blur, the pike snapped its jaws onto the small fish, my rod bent double in my hands, and a thrashing tail fin cut the surface of the water bubbling it up into raging white foam before my very eyes. It took a split second for me to gather my thoughts but while I was thinking them the pike suddenly dived taking the poor defenceless fish and my hopelessly inadequate line with it. I could feel the violent tugging as the pike made for the depths, I was forced to lower the rod and let the fish take some line…there was no way I was going to win this battle, my tackle was far too light (a size 14 hook, 3lb breaking strain line and of course, no trace*) any moment soon the pike would bite through the line and send me flying backwards over the chair at my feet…but that didn't happen…for some inexplicable reason I still had the beast on my line…and it wasn't letting go! This couldn't be happening, this David and Goliath battle did not make any sense, the odds were stacked heavily against me and yet I still managed to haul the fighting pike to the now turbulent surface. All of a sudden a crazy thought entered my head…I can land this fish, I could win this fight,…It was then that I turned my head briefly to see Linda standing behind me, obviously alerted by the splashing noises, a more than curious look on her face and the landing net lying close at her feet. "Quick, I screamed, grab the net, grab the net"

I could see the look of total confusion on her face but after following my excited gaze she bent over, picked up the landing net and was at my side in flash. She must have had a lot of practice in her childhood at hooking the plastic ducks from the little paddling pool at the fair because somehow she manage to scoop up the pike and hang on to the landing net pole even though the fish fought valiantly to get away. I dropped the rod onto the grassy bank and then took the net from her tired arms, we were both transfixed by the sight of the little monster in our midst and just stood for a while staring at it opened mouthed. It was then that we notice there were actually two fish in the net, one large snapping pike and one medium sized perch flipping about inches from its enormous mouth. The perch's backward facing spines had obviously caught in the bigger fish's mouth and the poor creature could not release it.

*Trace…a length of thin wire from line to treble hooks to prevent the teeth owning fish biting its way through ordinary nylon line.

No fish were hurt in the event of this anecdote…..

--- --- --- --- --- --- --- ---

"The hot water in the bathroom is running cold"

I was relaxing with a book in the cabin when her dulcet tones came to my ears on a wave of what sounded like growing frustration. I looked around at the water heater above the sink in the kitchen area and sure enough in the little aperture where there should have been controlled flames there were none. Also the sound coming from the water pump was not its usual rhythmic turning over but slow and intermittent, I put the book down, and made my way to the smallest room in the boat, further investigation was required.

The cold water on both the shower and the pedestal basin was running ok, the hot water to the shower was ok as was the hot water in the kitchen; the pedestal hot tap was no more than a dribble. I am no plumber but it was blatantly obvious to me that for some reason the water pressure from the water pump to the bathroom hot tap was insufficient to ignite the boiler. Something was amiss somewhere and it was up to me to find out what…I started to disconnect the piping to the hot tap in the small cupboard space below the basin…it was cramped, airless and hot…it was very soon to be a lot hotter….and a damn sight wetter!

As soon as I had the feed pipe freed from the tap, the pump kicked in and in doing so restored the water pressure fully to the boiler and igniting the gas …… in the dark and confined area and after banging my head on the base of the basin I was immediately treated to an impromptu shower of boiling hot water.

The Aftermath…..the tap itself was faulty, restricting the flow of water from the pump hence no heater response….but even more important than that was the fact that I'd forgotten to switch off the pump even before I got around to picking up a spanner…another lesson learnt the hard way.

Fire

It was a lovely Christmas evening…music playing in the Frenchgate centre Doncaster, crowds milling around happily, shop assistants were dressed as elves while we debated on a present for his mother – that was when the mobile phone call came…..'Oh Mrs Clover, I'm so glad I've got you….Bodhran's on fire….it's serious'

Linda had walked out of the store and was standing on the highly polished floor of the shopping malls huge concourse, her hand holding the mobile phone to her ear and a look of abject horror on her face….I was immediately aware that something terrible had happened and as I walked towards her, without saying a word, she handed the phone to me.

It was Sarah, the marina owner's daughter and she repeated to me what she had already said to Linda. All I really remember of our conversation was the words 'Bodhran, fire, serious' and that she would pick us up outside Doncaster Station as soon as possible.

Linda and I made our way down the escalator in a blind panic, all thoughts of Christmas shopping now totally forgotten, replaced with a heavy sickness in our stomachs and racing minds. "Does 'serious' mean her paintwork is badly spoilt, the awnings are now just steel skeletons covered with blackened and molten rags, she is a burnt out shell adrift in the marina?"...we did not know.

It might have been cold standing outside the station, it might have been pouring with rain, I have no recollection of any of that, it did not matter, all I can remember was that the thoughts that were going through my head were a rapid selection of scenarios, none of which held much hope for me.

It seemed Sarah would never get to us and the longer it took her the more time I had to convince myself that Linda and I's entire world had just gone up in smoke and we could do nothing about it.

 Sarah finally arrived and without preamble and with what shopping we had, we got in with it all humped on our laps, as we drew away from the kerb I found it almost impossible to say anything...and then Linda did...

I remember the beginning of the evening. Our first Christmas on Bodhran! I had decorated; we had a tree and tinsel hung from the curtain rails! We've had some lean years like every other family in Britain with a mortgage and children to raise, but now on our new life, no mortgage, no massive bills, this year we could really enjoy Christmas. I was so looking forward to present buying for children and grandchildren and with Evie, my granddaughter to indulge my inner child re; dolls and dressing up. I had so many plans and dreams of waking up on Bodhran on Christmas morning. Walking down the marina to shouts of 'Happy Christmas' and had rearranged my menus several enjoyable times! We intended after shopping to collapse in a pub for a meal, laden with packages and bags. The phone call came out of the blue, one minute we were part of a happy throng of people surrounded by happy faces and Christmas music. The next and I felt sick – I just wanted them all to get out of my way and to turn off that horribly happy music. As we stood outside Doncaster Station we did not talk. Joined in misery and panic I prayed to anything that may be listening – don't take my home away please, not now, not when I feel as if I have finally reached home. As we arrived back at the marina, for a minute I couldn't move. I didn't want to see what had happened to my home and I remember saying 'I don't want to see it' but I knew from somewhere that this would be the worst, get

that over and you move forward toward some sort of
normality. It was dreadful.

As we approached her moorings the first thing that we
were aware of was the awful reek of smoke, it filled the
air with a cloying, choking miasma which grew stronger
with every anxious step we took towards our home.
Although there were no visible signs on the exterior of
'Bodhran' (in the morning and in a better light we would
see the damage done to the funnel and the paintwork
surrounding it) we could see that the windows were
blackened and the blinds to the galley no longer in place.
We thanked Sarah for all she had done, declined her very
kind offer of an empty boat on the marina to avail
ourselves for the night and made our way to our pontoon
filled with a trepidation that was palatable.

The firemen had had to break down the stern door to
gain access to the fire; it was hanging off its hinges its
little round glass window in a million pieces on a carpet
that had been made sodden by the water hoses.
Although the bedroom and toilet area of the boat looked
relatively untouched (in a light that was rapidly fading
and struggling to penetrate the heavily sooted and
grimed windows) the main galley looked to be
completely gutted.

And the cause?....It would prove to be a very painful
learning curve for us both but hopefully a cautionary tale
for others....not only was the wood burner found to be
faulty, (an ill fitting door not readily visible) but a small

stack of dry wood left too close to the heat. Although we had shut down the burner prior to leaving the boat the wood was already hot and dry enough to self ignite. DO NOT STACK WOOD OR ANY OTHER COMBUSTABLE MATERIAL TOO CLOSE TO YOUR WOOD/COAL BURNER. We had of course fire and carbon monoxide alarms fitted and thanks to these and the firemen (and a neighbour's dog barking) the fire did not have time to completely destroy our home.

The main living area of Bodhran was blackened and ruined; my charred Christmas decorations added a pathetic touch and reminder of what we had lost. Everyone on the marina was so keen to help us and to tell us that it could be rescued, things would look better in the morning. The stench of burning was everywhere and stuck in my throat. Black and filthy water puddled throughout the boat. The windows were filled with black and yellow soot, with no power and little light there was nothing we could do so late in the evening. We locked up as best we could, thanked everyone for their help and Sarah as well for her offer of an empty boat for the night and headed to the Punch Bowl in town for a room and a drink.

I don't remember everything after that but I do remember arriving and booking a room. We left our meagre belongings in the room and headed for the bar. We ordered a drink and on realising their kitchen was nearly shut, a meal. Ham, egg and chips was actually an ironic reminder of happier times as this is Kim's only meal he can cook himself and he is always very proud to give me a break and cook dinner. We barely touched it. Something must have alerted us as Kim then explained what had happened and we realised that we had carried the smell of the boat with us arriving like a pair of overdone kippers! I will say here that we could not have had a better or more sympathetic reception than at the Punch Bowl and during our month long stay there the staff were amazing, took care of us so well and were so interested in how things were progressing. We had a few more drinks, a shower each, although we seemed unable to wash the burnt smell away, and fell into bed, where my dreams were full of fires, boats, running, being chased and more fires.

The morning brought with it the dread and dismay of realising that I hadn't just had a terrible nightmare, the smell emanating from my 'piled up on the floor' clothes reinforced it, Bodhran had been severely damaged. I don't think either of ate much of our breakfasts that morning and I for one had mixed emotions churning away in my stomach...*let's get to the marina as soon as possible....did I really want to see and smell the mess the fire had made of our new home?* We dressed in clothes that reeked of smoke and made our way to the marina.

I led the way along the pontoon and stepped aboard, the stench of the fire had not diminished at all and I was greeted by a freezing cold draught of smoky damp air as I pushed open what remained of our cabin door. Underfoot the carpet squelched rivulets of black water and with the benefit now of the light of day I could see it would be totally ruined – the least of my worries as it turned out.

The galley was an empty charred shell; the wood on the walls burnt, blackened and in some places completely gone with the insulation and metal beneath it clearly visible. All the window blinds had been destroyed, as was our small settee, pictures, television, table and light fittings. The glass in our bow doors had shattered and the wood in the metal surrounds gone. I stared for a long time at the big lump of plastic looking for all the world like a piece of liquorice toffee stuck on a wall before realising it used to be our clock!

All this, added to the ever present stench of smoke in the air, in our bedding, on our clothes and in the very pores of our skin could have easily put us off ever wanting to set foot in a narrow boat again...and to be honest, for a while it did more than just dent my enthusiasm...but Linda was having none of it, the sugar soap was out and we brought wire wool wholesale, she is obviously made of sterner stuff....and I thank God she is!

So the cleaning up began in earnest and our daughter–in–law Leann was there, wire wool in hand ready to do battle. First the windows had to be scrubbed clean of the sooty deposits that prevented daylight from getting through and then came the poignant task of sweeping away the remnants of what were our Christmas decorations, burnt to cinders and scattered all over the place. Interruptions to our endeavours were many but absolutely welcomed, people came from all over the marina offering help or bearing gifts, flowers, chocolates, wine – *'to help cheer you up'* – a foretaste to us of what boat people are really like.

We soon got our claim to the insurance people sanctioned, not only for the cost of repairs to the boat but also funds for us to stay at a local hotel until we were able to move back aboard. It was not possible for the work to be carried out at our marina so arrangements were made for us to take 'Bodders' to specialist boat repairers just down the canal where we were told "Mr and Mrs Clover I'll have your boat ready for Christmas if I have to work seven days a week" – (herein lies another story completely).

After an exhausting night's sleep I was glad to get going again, and we set out to see the damage in daylight and hopefully make a few steps towards getting our life back again. It was almost worse than I remembered – blackened and charred wood, soaking wet with puddles of filth everywhere. After clearing away the rubbish including all of our furniture, rug, carpets and bedding and the many years of our family's Christmas ornaments we were left with nothing more than a burnt hull. There was very little left of the home I had so proudly decorated. Leann took away with her most of our clothes and all remaining bedding and towels, I discovered afterwards that she had four loads of washing and it took three washes before they ceased smelling like a bonfire. The windows almost seemed an insult, blackened and a filthy yellow they were impossible to see through and I set too with a lot of sugar soap and elbow grease to open Bodhran up to the light again. It was then I really saw the boating community in action. So many people wanted to help, offering electric fires, boilers (someone had a spare!) and mostly an awful lot of chocolate. This, mainly from the women who recognised the importance of chocolate in an emergency as explained to me by another liveaboard, as she gave me a box of chocolates, a chocolate cake and two giant chocolate cookies! She said she just wanted to help make it better in some way!

After getting rid of some of my anger and making the windows at least look clean – whilst eating a lot of chocolate – I looked out our insurance documents. I remember a conversation I had with Sarah when we brought Bodhran mentioning one of the best insurance companies for narrow boats. You could find cheaper but they were always helpful in an emergency and generally good about paying out. I thank whoever is out there that we followed that advice, as they were wonderful! (Anyone requiring the company's name please contact us and we will gladly furnish you with it) One phone call and I was instantly given the name and contact number of the underwriters as they said it was easiest in an emergency like this. No waiting for signatures, our details taken over the phone we were told they would pay for us to stay somewhere up to the value of £1k whilst our boat was being repaired. Our quote was soon approved and we moved Bodhran to a new marina ten minutes away to be repaired and decorated. It was after we left her that I realised something – I did not have a home at that moment, nowhere to head to when I just wanted to collapse in my 'comfies' and shut out the world. I had not realised until that time how necessary my own space is to me. I have a strong nesting instinct and need my time alone, spent amongst my books and journals and now for the first time I had nowhere, only an impersonal room in a hotel. I thought the lack of Christmas decorations would upset me but I think what happened was so immense that Christmas didn't really matter. I remember saying to the people repairing Bodhran "I just want to go home and I can't" thank goodness for chocolate! Our boat repairers said they would do everything they could to get us back onboard. After a certain stage they would be happy to finish off around us but that was at least 3 or 4 weeks away.

We were now days away from Christmas and spending our daylight hours between Bodhran and the hotel. I found it difficult to stay any length of time in the boat as I felt awkward 'getting in the way of the man doing the work' - I found any excuse to be away whilst he got on with it. Linda on the other hand was still working, she would make herself a little bit of room somewhere on board and with laptop and coffee at hand, carry on. With no heating (the new wood burner was on order) and emergency lighting only, we spent our nights in the hotel.

Sometimes we would go away for a day or two only to come back to the boat and see that no further work had or appeared to have been done, it was an extremely frustrating feeling and as far as I was concerned it happened on far too many occasions – it became increasingly clearer that we were never going to be back aboard Bodhran before Christmas...alternative plans were going to have to be made and the wonderful invitations from our children to spend the Yule time period with them accepted.

The hotel staff could not have done more for us; they were amazing and always so interested in how things were coming along. Every trip back to Blue Water to get our post I would stand and gaze at the space where Bodhran should be and wonder when I would get back there.

We checked out of the hotel on Christmas Eve. We spent two days with our daughter's family and had a wonderful Christmas playing with the grand children; we spent a night with our eldest son and his wife playing cards. We went and visited Kim's family in Reading for a few days for a round of family parties and celebrations where I quietly envied them their homes and their family life untouched by the destruction of fire. Everyone made us so welcome. We returned for New Years Eve with our son and his wife saying goodbye to the old year and hoping the new one would see us finally back home. We had a wonderful time, but in the morning I found myself singing the chorus from the Paul Simon record' Homeless'! We left our sons house in Harrogate and headed over to the marina where Bodhran was being refitted. We had been told we could now move in if we wanted to and they would finish the rest around us. It was a freezing cold

January morning, there was no wood burner on board only a large electric fire they had lent us to dry out the boats flooring. We arrived back in time for the delivery of our new mattress and I set to unpacking and putting away our clothes and the clean linen and towels etc. washed by my daughter-in-law. I was home. It may have looked bare, the walls in the main living area were gone and only the outer steel shell showed, but we were home. There may have been no furniture and it may have been bitterly cold and icy, but we were home. I put the shopping away, put the kettle on and started to make up the bed. Kim looked about doubtfully,

"It's very cold"

"Yes"

I knew where he was going with this and I also knew it was going nowhere,

"Wouldn't we be better….."

"No"

"You didn't let me finish, I think….."

"We are not going to a hotel. I've spent over a week, sleeping in several different places, being a guest in other people's homes and I'm finally in my home!"

"I'm sure the bed is damp – one more night? We'd be better off in a hotel".

"It's a new mattress, the base was covered and was never damp and I'm not going to a hotel!"

"Where will we sit?"

"We've got two wooden picnic chairs and a foldable table"

"There's no T.V."

"I don't care about the T.V....I'm not going anywhere, I'm staying here"

Still looking at me doubtfully and now slightly exasperated he gave in realising that I had dug my heels in – I'd had enough, I was home and I was staying put!

That evening he went out for a drink, I'd been out enough to last me for years! It was dark so I lit a few candles. With no curtains I sat in the empty and shattered shell of the boat in my onesie, by candlelight and electric fire on a wooden folding chair with a glass of wine and I have never been happier.

Blue Water Marina is in the countryside and traffic is only heard distantly but you get birdsong all day, it is so peaceful, the boats are moored end on to the bank so you are sandwiched lengthwise on either side by other boats. At the new marina traffic was ever present as it was situated in the centre of town by the main road, but the boats were sideways on to the bank and you had a lovely view of the canal. As I sat there on our first night back I looked out at the town's lights reflecting on the water and wondered which was better!.....the view or the peace and quiet?....I am still undecided.

At last the interior work on Bodhran was well underway; a new wood burner had been ordered, the light fittings chosen, brass curtain rails and curtains picked out and purchased. We were offered new chairs for the lounge at a very reasonable cost (a kind and sympathetic gesture) from stock not used by the marina's boat builders and a visit to a large department store sorted out our lack of T.V. and other items destroyed by the fire. My main worry now was the saturated carpets in the aisle alongside the bedroom area leading to the lounge, caused no doubt by the firemen's hoses - well I thought it was my main worry until I ripped them all out and saw the damage beneath them! The water had seeped through the floorboards and between them and the boats metal structure had collected to about a quarter of an inch deep. I drilled out a small hole in the hope that it hadn't been able to find its way too far and was horrified to see with the aid of a pen torch that it had formed (as far as I was able to see) a small lake! I had two choices...take the entire floor out or try to pump the offending liquid out through the hole cut into the wood...either way it had to be done and the sooner the better....I chose the wrong option.

I started by drilling the existing hole out to half an inch and brought a small hand held plastic pump action siphon and a bigger more powerful torch. After an hour on my knees siphoning for all I was worth I finally got to the point where I had a washing -up bowl half full of (thankfully, for obvious reasons) clear water, red raw knees and no reflection from below when I shone my torch beam into the hole….eureka!...or for now at least it was… eureka….two hours later the waters reflection was back...it was smiling at me through the hole in the floorboards after its journey from somewhere else in the darkness of the boats subterranean structure! I was on my knees again. It was a recurring nightmare; I'd get to the point where there was no sign of any water and the metal surface below looked bone dry only to come back a few hours, and sometimes days later to see a fresh puddle had formed. Drastic action was needed. I drilled out four corners of a pencilled rectangle and fret sawed between them making the hole in the floorboards a neat 2"x 4". Further investigation (now obviously more thorough because the aperture was larger) with my torch beam revealed that below, the boards were indeed in sections, partitioned off by slats of 4"x4" timber….the water was trapped in these segments but as the boat moved it obviously found its way to the area in question….under my hole! I drilled further exploratory holes much further afield and found no sign of water anywhere else, which did a lot to encourage and cheer me up. I decided to bring in the big boys…

I disembowelled a plastic biro, broke off the wider end and taped it to the hose of Linda's shiny new mini vacuum cleaner making sure that the join was completely airtight. When the narrow end of the doctored biro was placed into the hole and the vacuum cleaner switched on the results were astounding...the water was sucked up as if by a very thirsty labrador after a 5 mile walk on a hot sunny day.

Using this method over a period of time and carrying out periodic checks the problem of the unwanted water was eventually solved. A few bouts with a small gas paint stripper had the damp wood dry in no time - but I was immediately faced with a whole new problem probably greater than the original one.....explaining to my dear wife why her shiny new vacuum cleaner no longer worked and why the guarantee on it would prove to be unquestionably invalid!

New flooring was the now the order of the day...we had always planned to take out the carpet (prior to the water damage) as it was a dull colour and lent nothing to the ambience of our home...cushion flooring and beading all along the edges now makes for easier cleaning and a brighter look.

We were very fortunate that the fire had not damaged the exterior of the boat or indeed the awnings – but an area around the chimney had been discoloured by the heat so I decided to paint the whole roof...it was a beautiful day and I have to report a strangely enjoyable chore once the masking tape was in place!

We soon settled into the day to day life of the new marina. I set up my laptop on the bed at one end of the boat whilst the work carried on at the other end. I missed my early morning walks in the peace and quiet but here there were other advantages. The toilets and showers were closer and as we were in town all the facilities were on hand, including a café just over the road that did takeaway bacon sandwiches if we had not had breakfast before work started. The only drawback was the everpresent traffic flowing right next to the marina – and the dog! One of the boats had a rescue dog that was, we were told, very friendly if you met it outside of the marina. Inside, and I soon realised it had not established its home boundaries yet and would let loose with blood curdling snaps, growls and barks whilst running full pelt towards the unfortunate person wandering along the

marina! I love dogs and they don't worry me (they do Kim), but even I began to feel very insecure if I found myself on open ground e.g. returning from the shower, and both Kim and I had made hasty and inelegant dashes to our boat to scramble from the bank to the safety of Bodhrans stern deck, just in time as the dog hared towards us! We had been assured that she would not do anything but we did not want to find out if that was correct.

Finally the day came! It was late January and still wintry when we untethered Bodhran and moved out into the canal for the return journey home, to Blue Water. We arrived back, moored up, connected ourselves to the electricity and looked around. We were home. The nightmare that had started on December 11th was finally over. I made a cup of tea and sat down to reflect on the last five or six weeks and look at the familiar view. I did miss being'sideways on' to the bank, I loved seeing the lights from houses reflected in the water, but here there was peace, quiet and tranquility (dogs leashed by order). The view of trees moving around us against the sky and birdsong all day was something I had really missed. We opened a bottle of bubbly in the evening to toast the end of our journey, but for me it was early the following morning when I clambered out of Bodhran and made my solitary way down the bank. It was so quiet. There was a freshness in the air and the light was winterbright in a blue sky. The birds were singing a dawn chorus and I knew I was finally home.

The fire had certainly put our original plans of 'going out' on the back burner and the repairs took a lot longer than we had envisaged, the warm summer days were getting shorter, the weather less favourable and going out for any distance or time, more problematic. Besides our 'landlocked commitments' had somehow bunched up and our free time all but gobbled up. Reluctantly the joint decision was made…it would be early next year before' Bodhran' would be cutting any worthwhile bow wave in the waters of Englands vast network of canals.

Repainted and refitted

Here we are, moored up to top up Bodhran's diesel tank.

Come with us for a few days cruising...

The weather for the next few days looked promising, warm and sunny with no mention of gales or heavy rain (nothing worse than fighting the winds when tying up for locks and moorings etc.). We'd popped out for extra rations i.e. milk, bread, tea and wine... (all the essentials!) - so come the morning all preparations made, we'd be off - or so we thought we would!

Later that evening word around the marina had reached us that the first lock in our journey (less than half a mile away) was broken and impassable...a quick check on-line confirmed it...a collar had become jammed and would need replacing...it would take at least two days. It was a pleasant evening so Linda and I decided to walk to the offending lock and see the damage for ourselves... The fact that the lock was situated right next to a rather lovely pub had I agree a slight influence on our decision to do so.

This was the sight that greeted us......

A quick drink in the pub to console ourselves was the order of the day and it had a calming effect on my irritation at not being able to set off the following morning. There was nothing more to do than to accept the fact, go back to Bodhran and await further news. The lock was actually repaired and ready to use midday the following day.

I find it almost impossible to carry on writing about our life living in a community on the marina without mentioning *'The Brothers'*…. elderly siblings that *'tired of the hustle and bustle of town living'* and settled together on their 'wide beam'. Fourteen years afloat they are the font of all knowledge when it comes to narrow boats, canals and the upkeep and maintenance of both. I have no doubt that every marina has its characters, its eccentrics, but we have been blessed twofold. At any time during the daylight hours (and it has been proven the night hours) one or both of 'the brothers' can be seen patrolling the marina – indeed it is their unwritten duty to close and lock the huge barriers at its entrance at the given times. Nothing is too much trouble for these men and I believe they derive a great deal of pleasure in helping out in any way they can, added to that they are visibly offended if any recompense or reward is offered.

A typical example of their desire to be 'of use and helpful:

On receiving news that the lock had been repaired we informed 'the brothers' that we intended to be going 'out' later and as we were doing just that we gave them both a little wave on leaving the narrow entrance out of the marina, they waved back. On approaching our first road bridge about a mile up the canal it was obvious that the way was clear for us to go straight through....on the side of the road frantically waving at us to do just that were the brothers –they had raced ahead of us through the town on their bicycles and had the bridge open and up as soon as we were sighted – we were free to cruise under it without even slowing down!'

It has been my experience that for various reasons more women tend to 'do the locks' than men. Given the nature of the job and the sheer physical strength needed to open some of the more antiquated and dilapidated of them you would suppose that it was generally a 'man's job' (no sexism intended). But no, watch a narrow boat approach the landing stage of the lock and invariably it will be a female crew member who steps onto terra firma first, windlass in hand ready to do battle. On some occasions of course where a lock is known to be extra stubborn or particularly 'worn out' I will moor Bodders, secure her and grab a second windlass to lend a hand.

It is usually the man who navigates into the lock and out again dropping off and picking up the 'lock/bridge opener' en route. I hasten to add this is a generalisation and by no means fact – I can only speak as I find!

I had definitely been the major force behind our move to our narrow boat Bodhran, but when it came to taking her out I was equally definitely not as enthusiastic as Kim. I loved living on her; I loved the way of life and the peace of the marina. The idea of controlling a thirteen ton, 45ft by 10ft cigar shaped narrow boat down a thin strip of water, passing other narrow boats – not to mention in and out of locks where we ran the risk of catching the cill and sinking her – did not appeal. Kim had all the courage in this area. We decided for our maiden voyage this year to head for Barnby Dun on the Stainforth and Keadby Canal. This involved turning right out of the marina and going through three swing bridges of various sizes and one lock before mooring up by a large low cantilever road bridge near water, toilet and shower facilities and with shops and pubs within walking distance. Kim knew I was nervous...we'd been out lots of time before on other narrow boats so I can only put it down to the fire and the realisation that 'Bodhran' had nearly been lost to us. I could not bear that thought and whilst we were moored up both she and I were safe! We made all our preparations; filled up with water, emptied the loo, stocked up with toilet fluid, candles, matches, wine, and some easy meals. I was smiling and confident to everyone but when the day came and a smiling Kim started unplugging the electric cable I found myself suggesting a trip by car to his family in Reading instead? No? How about Greece? The Canaries? We could be on a plane tonight if I rang up! There was no interest, he untied the ropes and we slipped from our moorings.

We took our usual places on the stern deck, Kim steering, me in front of the tiller ready with suggestions and 'tweaks' where necessary. Our marina is not the easiest to navigate but we made it out with no bumps at all! People waved as we left and I began to relax and enjoy the feeling of openness and freedom at being on the water again. The first bridge is in the centre of town with only a tiny stage to moor up and I was not looking forward to launching myself at the ground so I could go up and operate it. The brothers had got there before us and surrounded by children waiting to cross waved us through – another example of the community here! A two minute cruise and we reached the newly repaired lock. This is different to most locks I have seen being a mixture of lock and swing bridge and operated by a positive array of buttons.

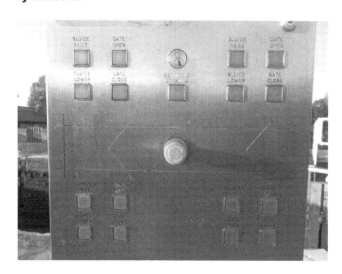

I was now frantically repeating "sluices up...gates open...boat in...gates closed...sluices down....." however when we got there and moored up we found the men from the Canal and River Trust still in attendance and working the lock to check its operation. They waved us through. I was enjoying this and just hoped our luck continued!

Following this lock is one of my favourite parts of this journey. A long, leisurely meander takes you through fields and woods, under bridges, past cows and horses and you see a part of the countryside usually hidden from view. I took lots of photos until Kim commented that we didn't need to see another photo of another field.

Under the motorway with the lorries whizzing past
above you and you feel as if you are in another world!

I made a coffee and took over steering for a while until a boat appeared in the distance I returned the tiller to Kim as problems with my eyesight mean I am sometimes unsure of our position in relation to another vessel – we're much safer with Kim!

The next obstacle is a small swing bridge – all bridges are operated using a British Waterways key that can also be used to access any facilities at locks such as toilets, showers and sluice. Having 'sailed through' the first two locks and bridges I was aware that this time we would not be so lucky. Since the fire and the refit that followed we had not been out far on Bodhran but it all soon became very familiar. The instructions on the road bridges are very clear and you cannot rush the operation. Indeed trying to rush it can cause the whole thing to freeze causing more delay to the drivers now viewing me

impatiently. I rejoined Kim on Bodhran after letting another narrow boat through the bridge ahead of us and we made our way to the next lock. The narrow boat we had let through had opened the lock and we made our way in but as sometimes happens things went wrong! Bodhran seemed very skittish and determined not to behave. Whatever we did she was caught by the increasing winds and we struggled to right her. This was not helped by the' Sergeant Major' style barked instructions by the skipper of the other vessel. Finally settled I climbed the ladder from inside the lock to assist in its opening – again accompanied by more instructions on how to open a lock! The other vessel moored up on the exit stage to the lock and I jumped 'literally' back on board Bodhran, but with some difficulty. The wind was now very strong outside the lock and we do not have bow thrusters helping us (unlike the other boat!). I landed on board behind the tiller and made my was crab-like to the stern with more shouted instructions following us and being thankfully blown away.

We travelled a short while, past the permanent moorings to an open stretch of canal and decided to moor up. I held Bodhran's rope mid ship while Kim got the mooring pins out until a lovely man who was just passing told us about the oil tanker that passes here regularly. Apparently, it also regularly pulls out all mooring pins setting vessels floating free with the strength of its bow waves and he suggested we moor up to the iron girder at the edge of the bank. You do meet some lovely people out boating!

We suddenly realised that dusk was approaching and we hadn't eaten since a late breakfast. We consulted the invaluable 'First Mates Guide' for the nearest shop and Kim set off. He loves walking and finds his relaxation that way. I decided it was wine o clock and with glass and Kindle sat in the bow to read, sip and enjoy the growing darkness, the sounds of the water and the echoing birdsong - which is generally my preferred way to relax!

Kim had noticed on his recce yesterday that five minutes ahead of us around a curve was a stretch of canal with bollards available for boats to moor up at for up to 48hours. It had toilets, showers, sluice; rubbish disposal points and was near to shops and pubs so the following morning we set off up river. We moored up in a lovely spot near fields a church and a lift bridge that provided us with an excellent opportunity to study other boaters mooring and steering!

I love being on the marina, it is 'home', but there is something special about being moored up completely alone, sideways onto the bank (as opposed to stern or bow onto the bank with boats either side) watching the sky darken chatting quietly as night settles and different sounds, calls and splashes echo all around you. Deciding to go inside and locking and bolting doors, closing curtains, lighting candles and enjoying a nightcap.

A handy bench beside us on the canal bank provided an ideal perch for breakfast on a beautiful sunny morning. We topped up our provisions at the local shop and decided to spend 20 minutes exploring a local church recommended in a Canal Guide. We were very lucky as it was cleaning day and an elderly couple of parishioners let us in. It was a medieval church with some stunning carvings and the wife of the couple pointed out items of interest to me. On hearing we lived on a narrow boat she exclaimed that she really envied me! It sounded such an idyllic life to her,' lying in a chair on board whilst the boat meandered along, nothing to do '– I certainly didn't have churches to clean! She must have seen my face as I thought of the last day or so jumping off Bodhran and launching myself at the canal bank to open a bridge or lock, heaving on a windlass and putting my back into opening a lock paddle as she said quickly 'I know you have locks to do, but still a very peaceful life' and in some ways she is quite right!

We spent a couple of days moored up there. Our daughter and her family came and found us (by road) for a party on Kim's birthday with our grand children fascinated that we had' 'floated' there – to a new place!

We found a lovely eclectic pub full of statues, figures, pictures and strange memorabilia and had a wonderful meal in a restaurant before walking home in torrential rain. We could not have got wetter, but after changing into dry clothes and sitting in the boat with a glass of wine, candles lit, rain drumming on the roof I am always struck by how cosy and peaceful my life can be.

The following morning we went through our usual chores; filling water, emptying the toilet, securing things that may fall down and readying ourselves for the journey home.

As that part of the canal was not particularly wide, we had decided to turn Bodhran by untying her ropes, all apart from the stern rope which would remain firmly attached to the bank, when, assisted by the wind and Kim with the barge pole we hoped she would simply float round, we should have known better! Untied, at any other time Bodhran would instantly float away whether we wanted her to or not, but now she remained as close to the bank as if still tied up and Kim was unable to 'pole' her around due to the depth of water. We were lucky. A couple of seasoned narrow boat owners walked passed, walking their dog and with a mixture of their help, my steering, Kim's poling at the bank we were soon heading back in the right direction with many shouted calls of thanks.

After the chaos of the final lock on our outward journey I was determined not to be fazed or rushed but to complete the lock methodically and steadily. This time it went perfectly! There was no one to shout orders or to confuse us and it was text book. Opening a lock involves much too-ing and fro-ing across the lock to open and then close each side. It is always easier if someone helps you, but in this instance I was happy alone. Except....as I re-crossed the lock for the umpteenth time crossing by the closed gate I was aware of the man sitting at the door of the boat nearest to me and studying my every move. I have no doubt if I had made a mistake his shouts would have alerted me. I ignored him and continued as he lent forwards making no attempt now to hide his focused stare on my actions and also making no attempt to help me at all.

We completed the other bridges perfectly culminating in some different men from the Canal and River Trust working the main lock in town as it was having problems again.

Despite some misgivings – working from the boat I have seen many boats trying to moor up in our marinas very limited space – but we managed it easily, backwards and forwards, backwards and forwards we inched into our home moorings (you cannot steer a narrow boat in reverse) it was lovely to be back and now we had memories of taking Bodhran out, manoeuvring her through locks and bridges. I know Kim felt differently about her following our trip, felt she was more 'ours' and more positive about our life on board!

It wasn't long after our little cruise that we were given some really exciting news, a 'garden moorings' had become available and (if Bodders would fit!!) we would be offered it. We had previously asked for the chance of such a move but this type of mooring is much sought after and in short supply. Pontoon mooring is all very well but it has its limitations as far as privacy, manoeuvrability (certainly in our case where our marina was so 'tight and less room to 'spread out'). Whereas as it name suggests, a garden mooring is sideways onto the canal, comes with the piece of land equivalent to your boats length and in most cases completely private and enclosed.

There was a suggestion that this particular mooring would be a few feet too short and with a slight curve in it unsuitable, so with a piece of nylon cord cut to the exact length of Bodhran, Linda and I went haring down a narrow alleyway between moored boats and a low wall to its location a few hundred yards away.

It didn't look promising; it appeared there'd be only inches to spare.

"I'll get you in" came the cry of one of the ever present brothers, "there's plenty of room, I'll get you in" – he must have seen the disappointed look on our faces because he went off striding back towards our boat without us, a man on a mission.

Together we slipped Bodhran's mooring ropes and disconnected our electricity lead and without too much hope started her engine for the short journey out of the marina's confines and down the canal.

With bow in and stern ropes thrown to land and secured with mooring pins it soon became obvious, much to our utter delight, that the brother (14 years a narrow boat man) had been right all along, Bodhran was 'in' with room to spare. We were now the new owners of an apple tree, a Christmas tree and a secured lawned garden with plenty of room for our bench set, storage shed and...an item of exceptional importance given our remote location, a newly purchased wheel barrow. It was not long (in fact the very day we moored up) that we got to know our next door boat neighbours both at stern and bow (as I have stated on numerous occasions in this book, you would be hard pressed to find a more friendly environment than the one of 'boaters').

'Bodders' now securely moored up we were left with the *'simple'* task of moving our land -bound bits and pieces (i.e. storage shed, bench set, etc.etc.) to our new domain which turned out to be easier said than done. It was a blisteringly hot day and the narrow gravelled path (260 steps, I counted them!) leading to our new moorings was nowhere near wide enough to allow our van through – it was barely wide enough for us and had to be single file all the way. Everything we moved had to be either loaded into the wheelbarrow or dismantled and pulled along in a steel trolley which was kindly leant to us by our new neighbours.

Firstly we emptied the 'shed' containing all our bags of stored winter clothing, photo albums, suit cases, shoes, pictures, books and numerous 'other things retained but without room for onboard'. Many trips were made back and forth with loaded wheel barrow, knuckles scraped against the low walls of the alley and curses flying as things fell off which had to be retrieved after being 'jammed' in its the front wheel. Once all the contents of the 'shed' had been relocated it was time for the shed itself - being of plastic and aluminium construction 5ft tall, 6ft wide and 3ft deep it was not excessively heavy more cumbersome, which was not helped by it being balanced on top of the trolley. Less than a quarter of the way along and it was obvious to us both that due to a number of obstacles in and alongside the alley we were not going to make it without lifting the thing above wall height and carrying it. We got no more than three steps forward before Linda nearly tripped on the gravel, lost her hold on the shed and it toppled over. We were left with the shed angled precariously atop the low wall, its lid opened and jammed between the thin branches of a privet hedge and me stranded between it and the redundant trolley, we were going nowhere fast.

And then we heard *'the voice'*, the voice of an angel

"Do you need a hand with that guys?"

It was yet another boat neighbour on his way up the alley behind us, willing and wanting to lend a helping hand so with his help and Linda's guidance at the lead, we carried the shed the rest of the way to its new place in our garden. The easy part of the move was over!!

The garden bench set was 'thankfully' the last of our possessions to be moved and as you can probably gauge from the above picture fine for sitting on 'glass in hand' but of heavy construction and of course considerable weight. 'Not a problem' I announced to no-one in particular as I went in search of my socket set – in a few minutes I will have it taken down and in manageable sections for transit bit by bit on our borrowed trolley. I had put it together I could easily take it apart. Wrong. The nuts were all of the locking type with nylon inserts, the bolt heads flushed or in some cases sunken into the woods surface- when I set the socket to the nuts and applied force the whole lot turned squeaking in the hole but stubbornly stayed exactly where it was...after a lot of chin stroking and shaking of the head I realised I would have to get the 'big boys' out.

I hadn't used the portable angle grinder for a good many years and I wasn't even sure if I had any suitable cutters – I was more than happy when I saw I had two or three unused ones lying in the bottom of the toolbox still packaged. I would cut slots into the heads of the bolts and use a screwdriver to hold them fast whilst removing the nuts. It worked, slowly but surely I unscrewed the necessary bolts and Linda and I hauled the bench to our new home heavy bit by heavy bit.

An hour or two later our bench set was back together and standing proud in our new garden under the weight of a bottle of wine and two glasses – it was back breaking work and we both felt we'd earned a rest. And that's when the voice of our new neighbour came floating over from his side of his garden.

"Hey guys, I hope you don't think I'm being rude, but why didn't bring your bench set up here on the roof of your boat?"

We poured ourselves another drink.

With the approach of autumn we settled back into life at the marina and after a few discussions and a bit of luck we were offered a much prized 'garden mooring'. These are reached by a narrow gravel path bordered by hedges and a low wall and consisted of the boats being 'sideways on' to the bank next to their own private enclosed garden. I loved it! With the help of the brothers, on a sunny morning we were soon tied up at our new home which for me held the best of everything in this life. A permanent view of the water the length of our boat, the open sky, sunrise, and the colourful sunsets now could be fully enjoyed and become part of our world. On our first full day there I sat in our garden read a book, did some knitting, had a cup of tea – and in complete privacy. Don't get me wrong, I love being part of this community, but it is lovely to tuck yourself away and have your own space outside to do so, without being on permanent display.

I had thought that as we moved our 'home' and I hadn't had to empty any cupboards that moving would be easy! I was wrong. We are some distance from our old mooring – from one end of the marina to the other – and after about the twentieth journey backwards and forwards with a filled wheel barrow or kindly lent trailer from a new neighbour I was exhausted. As liveaboards we do tend to spread onto the surrounding area and we had a lot to transport. At 7pm. (some eight hours later!) Kim decided we should finish with the table and bench set. I followed him (again) to our old home and got left behind. He reached the table, turned, watched me limp exhaustedly after him and I think realised I had had it. When I reached him he suggested a glass or two of wine in our new garden and leaving the rest until tomorrow. It was bliss!

So here we are…. It took around two years but we finally have the life I envisaged all that time ago. We are next to the bank with an open view of water, fields and sky. As I sit here now it is October and the darker evenings are creeping in. The wood burner is lit giving a cosy glow to the evening and the only sound is the crows calling to one another and occasional duck. Cygnets were practising 'take –off' earlier amid much splashing and a Heron has been sighted on the bank opposite us. I do love it here.

So here we are….if someone had said to me five years ago that I'd be living on a narrow boat, quite happy about leaving terra firma behind and spending the majority of my time afloat …I would have asked the barman to have one of what that 'someone' was drinking.

It isn't a life to be looked at through rose tinted glasses any more than it's a life like a roll in the hay. It can be so cold on a winter's morning that you scrape ice from the inside of the windows, so hot in the summer that even with the said windows out and the bow doors wide open its hard to escape the heat. The toilet needs emptying, the water needs getting, the gas cylinders need replenishing, the fire needs tending, cleaning and rebuilding with coal and wood, the batteries need charging and sometimes just sometimes you wish that there were escape lanes in the galley so you could pass each other without ' bending backwards and breathing in'. In short it is a totally different life.

So if you are not prepared to rough it, to work at it, to extend yourself and learn and develop new skills...maybe it's not the life for you.

If on the other hand you enjoy your freedom and would cherish the chance to be able to 'up anchor and go' whenever the fancy came to you, if you want to live in a community where everybody is your equal, your friend, your shipmate, if you have no qualms about raising your hand and waving to your fellow narrow boaters as they pass you by in the middle of the canal in the middle of nowhere...then maybe someday we'll be waving at you. I hope so.

Printed in Great Britain
by Amazon